Revised and Updated

# Backroads of Ontario

## RON BROWN

# FIREFLY BOOKS

# A FIREFLY BOOK

Published by Firefly Books Ltd. 2013

First Printing

**Publisher Cataloging-in-Publication Data (U.S.)**
Brown, Ron, 1945–
    Backroads of Ontario / Ron Brown.
Originally published: Erin, Ont., Boston Mills Press, 2003.
[224] p. : col. photos. ;  cm.
Includes index.
Summary: This guidebook features 22 trips, each illustrated with photographs and accompanied by an easy-to-follow map. Trips range in length from afternoon outings to weekend excursions; all lead to out-of-the-way places within easy driving distance of major cities in Ontario.
ISBN-13: 978-1-77085-241-9  (pbk.)
1. Ontario—Guidebooks.  2. Automobile travel—Ontario—Guidebooks.  3. Rural roads—Ontario—Guidebooks.
917.1304/4 dc23      F1057.7.B768 2013

**Library and Archives Canada Cataloguing in Publication**
Brown, Ron, 1945–
    Backroads of Ontario / Ron Brown.—Rev. ed.
ISBN 978-1-77085-241-9
    1. Rural roads—Ontario—Guidebooks.
2. Ontario—Guidebooks.  I. Title.
FC3067.6.B76 2013      917.1304'5      C2013-901227-3

Published in the United States by
Firefly Books (U.S.) Inc.
P.O. Box 1338, Ellicott Station
Buffalo, New York  14205

Published in Canada in 1996, 2003 by Boston Mills Press

Published in Canada in 2013 by
Firefly Books Ltd.
50 Staples Avenue, Unit 1
Richmond Hill, Ontario L4B 0A7

Cover and Interior design:
Gareth Lind, LINDdesign

Printed in Canada

*The publisher gratefully acknowledges the financial support for our publishing program by the Government of Canada through the Canada Book Fund as administered by the Department of Canadian Heritage.*

**Opposite: Inglis Falls Conservation Area near Owen Sound.**

# Contents

**A lookout point on Manitoulin Island. See Route 19.**

# The Story of Ontario's Backroads

*The road was scarcely passable; there were no longer cheerful farms and clearings, but the dark pine forest and the rank swamp crossed by those terrific corduroy paths (my bones ache at the mere recollection) and deep holes and pools of rotted vegetable matter mixed with water, black bottomless sloughs of despond! The very horses paused on the brink of some of these mud gulfs and trembled ere they made the plunge downwards. I set my teeth, screwed myself to my seat and commended myself to heaven.*

Today's backroad adventures are a far cry from 1837, when traveller Anna Jameson wrote the above words. Indeed, thanks to those who flee the hustle of freeways and the tedium of suburban sprawl to seek the tranquility of an uncluttered countryside, backroad driving is North America's most popular outdoor activity.

This book leads you from Ontario's main highways onto its backroads. Before 1939, the province had no expressways. That was the year King George VI and Queen Elizabeth opened the Queen Elizabeth Way. In 1929, Ontario had less than 2,000 km of hard-surface highway. Before 1789, it had no roads at all. European settlement of Ontario began with the arrival of the United Empire Loyalists from the war-torn colonies that had become the United States of America.

The Loyalists settled on the shorelines of the St. Lawrence River, Lake Ontario and Lake Erie, and they had no need of roads. But the governor of the day, John Graves Simcoe, casting a wary eye on the restless neighbour to the south, embarked on the building of military roads. In 1793 he ordered a road from Montreal to Kingston, and Ontario soon had its first road. (You can follow it even today as County Road 18 through Glengarry County.) This he followed with Yonge Street and Dundas Street, which also survive and have retained their names.

Despite the slow pace of settlement through the early years of the 19th century, the pattern of Ontario's road system was taking shape. From the Loyalist ports roads led inland to bring out lumber and farm products. They were useless quagmires in spring and little better in summer. Only in winter, when frost and snow combined to create a surface that was hard and smooth, did farmers haul their wheat to port.

Settlement roads connected the main towns of the day. Among the more important were the Danforth Road, replaced soon after by the Kingston Road (portions of both survive), linking York (now Toronto) with Kingston; the Talbot Trail that followed the shores of Lake Erie; and roads to the northwest, such as the Garafraxa Road, the Sydenham Road and Hurontario Street.

As settlement progressed, surveyors made their way through the forests, laying out townships and

Opposite: Indian Head at Ouimet Canyon Provincial Park near Dorion, Ontario — see Route 21.

Fall scenic highway in northern Ontario.

surveying each into a rigid grid of farm lots and concessions. Along each concession they set aside a road allowance, linked at intervals of 2 to 5 km by side roads. And so Ontario's road network became a checkerboard that paid no attention to mountains, lakes and swamps.

One of the first problems was that there was no one to build the roads. Although each settler was required to spend twelve days a year on road labour, settlers were few at first.

In the 1840s, the government turned road-building over to private companies and to municipalities. Some of the companies tried such improvements as macadam and planks. But rather

than being grades of crushed stone, the macadam was often little more than scattered boulders, while the planks rotted after a few years. When the railways burst on the scene in the 1850s, road companies and municipalities both turned their energies to railway-building.

Despite the railways, the government tried one more road-building venture, the colonization road scheme. This was in the 1850s, when lumber companies were anxious to harvest the pine forests that cloaked the highlands between the Ottawa River and Georgian Bay. Although early survey-ors had dismissed the agricultural potential of the upland of rock and swamp, the government touted the region as a utopia for land-hungry settlers. What the politicians didn't reveal was that the main aim of the scheme was to provide labour, horses and food for the timber companies. Once the forests were razed and the timber companies had gone, the settlers who had moved to the area were left to starve. By 1890 most of them had fled, and the roads in some cases were totally abandoned. Nevertheless, a few of them retain their pioneer appearance and have become some of the backroads in this book.

In 1894 the Ontario Good Roads Association was formed to lobby for better roads, and in 1901 the government passed the *Highway Improvement Act* to subsidize county roads. Finally, in 1915, the government got back into the business of road-building and created the Department of Highways. The first 60 km of provincial road was assumed east of Toronto in 1917.

But for decades afterward, northern Ontario remained railway country. Most towns and villages north of the French River owed their existence to the railways, and what roads there were stabbed out from the railway lines to the lumber and mining camps.

The years following the Second World War saw the arrival of the auto age, and during the 1950s and 1960s Ontario embarked on a spate of road improvements unequalled in the entire previous two centuries. Road-building continues unabated, and as it does it destroys much of the province's traditional landscape. As rows of maple and elm, cedar rail fences, and roadside buildings fall before the bulldozer, Ontario is left with a legacy of endless asphalt. Despite enlightened planning, countryside sprawl continues to engulf Ontario's once pastoral landscapes. It is not surprising, therefore, that Ontarians, overwhelmed with the tedium of an omnipresent suburbia, are travelling farther afield to seek the tranquility of backroad Ontario.

The backroads in this book are special. Each has a story of its own. Some follow the unhappy colonization roads, some the more prosperous settlement roads; some explore rural areas that have retained their century-old landscapes, others follow the shores of lakes or rivers. Some plunge into deep valleys and mount soaring plateaus. Others take you into northern Ontario to logging areas old and new, to once-booming silver fields and to the fringes of the province's last frontiers.

Although the maps at the start of the four major parts of the book, along with those that accompany the 22 that guide you through each chapter, contain basic information, you will also need to bring along more detailed road maps or a quality GPS device. And don't overlook the driving and walking tours offered by many local counties and municipalities.

# Section 1
# Southwestern Ontario

# 1 The Hidden Treasures of the Erie Shore Road

This route winds along Ontario's most underrated and perhaps most maligned shoreline, that of Lake Erie. Following a pioneer trail along the lake's shores and bluffs, it begins at Port Dover, 60 km southwest of Hamilton, and runs 95 km westward to Port Stanley.

This trip will delight the water lover, the birdwatcher and the history buff. Public wharves in most towns provide opportunities to cast for Lake Erie's popular yellow perch or to watch squat-fishing tugs chug to their berths. Here, too, are clifftop lookouts, more public than on any comparable length of Great Lakes shoreline, marshes that abound in bird and plant life, and some of Ontario's best-preserved early towns.

**Many of Port Dover's historic harbourside buildings have been preserved.**

Lake Erie's first settlements were founded by the United Empire Loyalists, refugees from America's post-revolutionary persecutions. But no sooner had they begun to get established than the War of 1812 burst upon them, bringing with it a devastating raid that laid waste to farms, homes and industries. However, settlement revived after the war, spurred on by Thomas Talbot, a retired army officer who sold his land grants to any settler meeting his stringent standards. Busy villages developed around the mills and small harbours, and, as the homesteaders moved up the creeks and crude trails, the backlands began to fill. The railway age ushered in even greater prosperity to those towns fortunate enough to be on a rail line. The little ports thrived and the fishery flourished. Then, in the 1920s, just as farming appeared to be declining, tobacco crops were introduced to the infertile sands and gave agriculture a much-needed boost.

## Port Dover

Port Dover, the start of this route, was until recently Ontario's fishing capital and the home of the world's largest freshwater fishing fleet. (That fleet now calls Wheatley, Ontario, home.) It began as a mill town called Dover Mills, but in 1812, as the Yankee invaders ignited their fiery trail across the countryside, Dover Mills was reduced to ashes. To take advantage of the growing trade in lumber and grain, the townspeople rebuilt closer to the lake. Later, after the coming of the railways, commercial fishing boomed and Port Dover grew quickly. Most of the town's historic buildings date from those heady years in the late 19th century.

The town has several fascinating sights, and most of them can be seen on foot. If you follow St. Andrew Street from Highway 6 to Harbour Street, you will come to the Port Dover Harbour Museum. Housed in a restored fisherman's shanty, built about 1890, it displays old-time fishing equipment and graphically depicts the tribulations of fishing on Lake Erie.

Farther along the west side of the harbour, the former net sheds and shanties of the old fishermen's quarter have become homes, craft shops and restaurants. At the end of the street, you come to the public wharf. No matter when you visit, you will see local residents casting a line in the water or just watching the fishing tugs glide behind the breakwater and manoeuvre for space in the more recent harbour on the east side.

## Port Dover to Normandale

To leave Port Dover, turn left from Highway 6 onto Nelson Street at the north end of the commercial core. This part of the route is marked by signs announcing the "Talbot Trail." For the first 2 km the route treats you to bluff-top views over Lake Erie; then it heads inland across a flat farmland of pastures, orchards and a few commercial greenhouses. After 6 km turn left at Port Ryerse Road, and 2 km farther on you will come to Port Ryerse.

Named for Colonel Sam Ryerse, an early mill owner, this wooded narrow gully has gone from busy shipping centre to quiet cottage community, and it has some of the oldest buildings on Lake Erie. Atop the east side of the gully stands the picturesque white frame Memorial Anglican Church, c.1869. The church has witnessed many changes, as has a large brick hilltop mansion, the former Ryerse family home.

Your next stop after Port Ryerse will be another former centre of activity, Normandale. To get there, continue 1 km west until you come to a fork in the road. Keep left on Front Road, a winding farm road, and, after 5 km, you will come to a T intersection. Turn left, and, after about half a kilometre, you will be in the cottage community of Fishers Glen. Once in this wooded gully, keep

right, drive 2 km to a T intersection; turn left and drive less than 1 km to Normandale.

## Normandale

As you descend the hill into this quiet valley, you may find it hard to refer to Normandale as "yesterday's Hamilton." Yet for three decades in the 19th century, Normandale was Ontario's foremost iron producer, thanks to Joseph Van Norman. The production of iron was launched here in 1815 by John Mason, who simply burned a mixture of charcoal and bog ore from the many local swamps. Van Norman acquired the operation in 1828 and turned it into a major industry.

A town plot of five streets and 42 lots was laid out, and by 1846 the town had a population of 300, a gristmill, and a main street full of businesses. However, by 1848 the timber and ore were gone. Joseph Van Norman moved on, and Normandale became a ghost town. Today it exists as a cottage and country-living community.

Yet you may still see vestiges of its glory years. At the foot of the hill is a T intersection where, on the southeast corner you will see a two-storey frame building with a front gable. This is the former Union Hotel built by Van Norman himself, and it has been restored. Adjacent to it, the small building with the "boomtown" facade served as the village post office. Near the lake, down Mill Lane, lies the site of Van Norman's foundry, commemorated by a historical plaque. So thoroughly was the industry abandoned that Van Norman's blast furnaces lay buried and forgotten until their rediscovery by Royal Ontario Museum archaeologists in 1968. One of the furnaces is now in Upper Canada Village in eastern Ontario, and the other is in the Eva Brook Donly Museum in Simcoe, just 17 km north of Normandale on Highway 24.

The water-powered Backus Mill near Port Rowan is Ontario's oldest.

## Normandale to St. Williams

To continue on the pioneer trail, drive west from the Union Hotel up the wall of the gully and, after 1 km, stay left on Front Road. This scenic section of the route winds through woods and fields for 1 km to a stop sign at Regional Road 10. South of the intersection, at the foot of Lake Erie's cliffs, lies Turkey Point. Atop the bluff a golf course covers the sites of Fort Norfolk and Charlotteville. They were built as a fortified administrative district seat during the last decade of the 18th century, when the threat of an American invasion loomed large. But the fort was never finished and instead the district seat was relocated to Vittoria, a safer inland location. Charlotteville and Fort Norfolk quickly vanished from the landscape, and today only a historical plaque marks the spot. Turkey Point is a peninsula of shifting sand which extends 5 km

into the lake and encloses a vast marsh. A popular public beach lines the lake.

As you drive west from Regional Road 10, the trees of a forest form a leafy tunnel. About 3 km from Regional Road 10, the route skirts a high bluff offering a vista across the grassy Turkey Point marsh to the wooded spit beyond. Here, too, you pass fields that are flat and sandy, with long rows of leafy crops and lined with square wooden barns painted green and red. This is Ontario's tobacco country and one of Canada's richest agricultural communities. Yet a little over half a century ago it was a wasteland.

Originally, Norfolk's sand plains, as they are called, were a park-like savannah of oaks and grasses. The first settlers, attracted by the light, stone-free soils, quickly cleared the area of its sparse forest. However, a few bountiful crops

**Cliffs of clay mark the Lake Erie shore near Port Bruce.**

depleted the soil, and, one by one, the farms were abandoned, leaving Norfolk a desert of blowing sand, good for little other than pine plantations. Then, in 1923, agricultural scientists Henry Freeman and William Pelton carefully studied the soils and decided to introduce tobacco. Their foresight paid off, and Norfolk became Canada's leading tobacco region. However, high cigarette prices and the growing concern over tobacco-induced cancer have once more sent the area into an economic downspin. A few former tobacco producers have begun planting peanuts and ginseng, while others have reverted to more traditional crops such as wheat and oats.

## St. Williams

From the cliff-top the road ventures inland through the periphery of tobacco country and,

after 5 km, stops at the farm village of St. Williams. This community was originally called Neals Corner but the name was changed to honour William Gellassy, a local landowner and religious leader. Located just 1 km from the lake, St. Williams was in its early years a shipping and milling centre. But with the arrival of the South Norfolk Railway and, later, the growth of the tobacco industry, it became a busy farm-service town of about 200. Although it is quieter now and many of its early businesses have folded, you can still find a few older houses and a church from those heady times.

## St. Williams to Port Rowan

At the stop sign, turn left, drive a few metres and turn right. For 5 km this road winds through the farm fields and along the cliff to the busy resort town of Port Rowan. From the stop at County Road 42, the main street of Port Rowan lies to your right. A disastrous fire in 1919 destroyed most of the downtown area, leaving few historic buildings. At the north end, however, the blaze stopped short of the Baptist church, which stands as it has since 1856, with its white steeple rising above its brick walls.

The main attraction of Port Rowan is its shoreline. Turn left and descend the hill to the Lions Club Park, a small treed picnic area wedged between the harbour and a curving beach. Once a bustling port and fishing centre, the harbour is now home largely to pleasure craft.

From Port Rowan you can take a side trip to see Ontario's oldest mill. Follow County Road 42 north through the town for 3.5 km, and follow the signs to the Backus Heritage Conservation Area. The wooden mill that you see here was the only mill on Lake Erie to survive the scorched earth devastation of the American attack in 1812. It grinds grain today just as it has since it was built in 1798. The conservation area also offers 20 restored pioneer buildings, including an unusual octagonal schoolhouse that dates from 1866. You may also camp, fish or follow the 12 km nature trail through one of southern Ontario's most extensive Carolinian forests.

## Port Rowan to Port Burwell

Return to Port Rowan and follow County Road 42 through town and then carry on for 2 km until you arrive at a stop sign for Highway 59. Six km south lies Lake Erie's longest sand spit, Long Point, a 32 km finger of shifting sands and swampy channels that stabs into Lake Erie. A small provincial park is situated at the end of the highway, but most of the point is privately owned. Nevertheless, the peninsula is a major port of call for birdwatchers.

The next section of your route passes through a string of faded hamlets and long-gone schooner

ports—some that have come back to life as country living quarters and others that have vanished altogether. From Highway 59, continue west on County Road 42. After 2 km, you will come to a wide swampy inlet and a small string of houses, the village of Port Royal. The marshlands that now clog the creek belie its early role as a bustling schooner port.

From Port Royal, your route crosses an area of fertile farms until, after 8 km, a handful of buildings announces the former schooner port of Clear Creek. Once a busy lumber port, Clear Creek lost its unprotected wharf to Erie's waves after just a few decades.

Continue along County Road 42. After 4 km, a small range of hills looms on the left. Known as the Sand Hills, the ridge marks the sudden appearance of shoreline sand hills. A private park, the Sand Hills have camping and picnic facilities as well as a beach. For your best view of these remarkable sand cliffs, pay your park admission and follow the trail down the 100-metre-high sand pile to the beach.

For 14 km the road continues along the shore, passing through villages such as Jacksonburg, Houghton and Hemlock, as tobacco fields spread straight and flat into the distance.

## Port Burwell

Another of Erie's once busy ports, Port Burwell is quiet now, more popular for its beaches and its 1840 lighthouse that sits right in the middle of town. The marine museum displays an extensive nautical collection. In 2013, the Elgin Military Museum relocated here from St. Thomas and displays the submarine, Ojibwa.

A few fishing tugs still make Port Burwell their home and offer fish for sale. Cross the bridge and continue on County Road 42 where you can pause in Iroquois Beach Provincial Park for a swim or a stroll on one of Lake Erie's longest beaches.

## Port Burwell to Sparta

Continue west along County Road 42. Thanks to the shoreline's moderate climate, this is not only prime tobacco country but also greenhouse and orchard territory. Some of the peach and cherry orchards offer the opportunity to pick your own fruit; others have retail booths by the roadside.

For the next 17 km the road follows a straight line about 2 km inland. The farmland is flat and prairie-like. Prosperous rural communities such as Lakeview and Grovesend dot the route. Then, at County Road 73, County Road 42 ends. Turn left here, then follow the highway 3 km through a series of deep wooded gullies to the once busy Port Bruce.

Erosion has left a series of hills and gullies that were once the shore bluff. It was around these hills that the village grew. It too started as a lumber port and then boomed with the growth of commercial fishing. But Port Bruce never attracted a railway, and the fishermen soon moved on to ports that did. The cliffs and valleys, however, did not go unnoticed, and Port Bruce has become a popular cottage and recreation centre. Beside the river mouth is a small treed park, and the long sandy beach is now a provincial park.

To leave Port Bruce, follow County Road 73 back to the bridge and turn left onto County Road 24. For 4 km this road carries on past cliff-top views before it swings inland. After 2 km, watch for the intersection with County Road 36 and turn right. Drive along this road for 3.5 km and you will arrive in Sparta, Ontario's oldest and best-preserved Quaker village.

## Sparta

Although new homes have been built around Sparta, the original village core surrounding the main intersection has survived almost intact. On the southeast corner is the general store (now a

craft shop), which was built in 1842 of handmade bricks. On the northwest corner stands the old Sparta House Hotel, with its long wooden porch. It too was constructed in 1842, and stood empty for several years before receiving new life as a tea room. Next to it is the Forge and Anvil Museum and the old village smithy, but one with a difference: it was made from adobe brick. About 1 km west of the intersection stands one of Ontario's oldest and best examples of Quaker architecture, the Haight-Zavitz house. Indeed, much of the main street survives as it appeared a century ago, and it is proudly preserved. A short distance north of the intersection, the Quaker Meeting House still survives. You may pick up a walking-tour guide in almost any shop.

Return south along County Road 36 to County Road 24 and turn right. The flat, prosperous farmlands here seem endless. Farm homes, which might more appropriately be termed mansions, testify to the bounty. One outstanding example is just 2 km south of Sparta on the east side of the road.

After continuing west for 9 km on County Road 24, you will come to County Road 23. Follow this road a short distance to St. Joseph Street in Port Stanley and to the centre of town. Port Stanley is a town of 2,000 that still lives off shipping and the lake.

## Port Stanley

The area was first settled in 1818, several years after the shoreline farther east was opened. The harbour at Port Stanley was not ready until 1823, and the place remained a small shipping port until 1857, when the railway reached town. Built jointly by the counties of Middlesex and Elgin, the London, St. Thomas & Port Stanley Railway was one of Ontario's shortest lines.

Port Stanley is a fitting place to end this particular tour, a busy modern community that retains

**The memorial to Port Dover's fishermen.**

its historic links to the lake—and even to the railway—and harbours a rich collection of historic buildings. At the junction of Bridge and Main Streets you will find downtown Port Stanley, with its shops, taverns and restaurants. Main Street follows the east bank of the harbour, and along it are Port Stanley's oldest buildings. No. 211 is the Russell House, a brick inn constructed in the 1850s and later repurposed as a bank, a butcher's shop and offices. No. 207 is unarguably Port Stanley's most historic building, for it was built in 1822 by the town's founder, Colonel John Bostwick. Originally a warehouse, it is now a private home. Next to it stands a yellow brick house, considered by many to be the port's most handsome structure. It was built in 1873 by Manuel Payne, who served variously as postmaster, telephone operator and customs officer. Farther along are net sheds,

ice-houses and other buildings from the early days of fishing.

On the west side of the bridge, you will find the efforts of local railway enthusiasts to keep alive the community's railway links. The station for the Port Stanley Terminal Railway is the point of embarkation for rail excursions to the southern outskirts of St. Thomas.

It is wise to pick up a brochure that guides you on a walking tour of the place and then meander along the beach, enjoy a meal or perhaps even stay overnight.

To return home via Highway 401, simply follow Highway 4 north from Port Stanley to its junction with that freeway.

# 2 The Tranquility of the Grand River Road

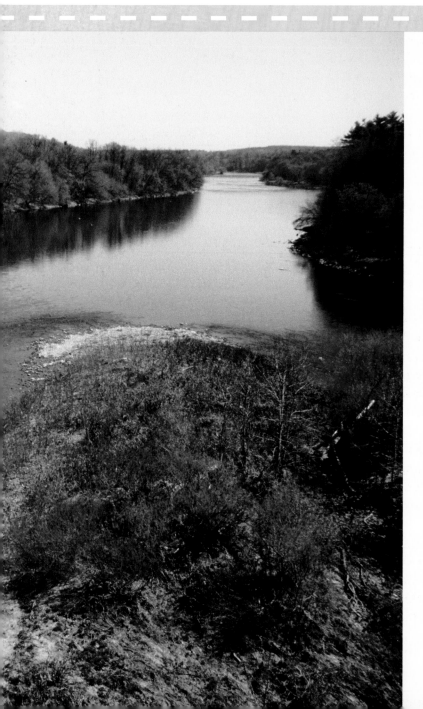

The Grand River is one of Ontario's most historic water-ways. From its humble swampy beginnings far to the north of Kitchener, it rushes through a rock-walled canyon at Elora before meandering through a gentle countryside to its outlet into Lake Erie.

This route follows the portion south of Brantford—that is, the most historic part of the river. Here, the Grand's links to the First Nations are the strongest, and here it was tamed and confined between the walls of a long-forgotten canal.

The route is relatively short, requiring a mere half-day, and should appeal to almost every-one. It offers history and Native lore, handsome 19th-century homes and mills, and opportu-nities to fish, photograph or just relax in a riverside park.

**The valley of the Grand River near Brantford.**

The story of the Grand River reflects the frustrations of Ontario's Native peoples as few others do. In 1784, Mohawk Chief Joseph Brant and his Six Nations followers from New York State were granted all the lands along the river as a reward for having fought and died beside the British in several valiant victories in the American Revolutionary War. But when settlers made their way up the Grand, clamouring for land, the British began to reduce Brant's holdings. Today, Brant's descendants retain a fraction of that land.

Settlement remained light, however, until 1829, when William Merritt and Absalom Shade decided to construct a canal along the Grand and pressured for even more of the Native lands. The first ships passed through the canal in 1835, and lock-side towns soon burst into life. Sawmills and gristmills flourished. But during the 1850s, as railways began to snake their way across the countryside, river traffic dwindled. The last vessel passed through the locks in 1890, only 55 years after the waterway was first opened. An era had quickly passed.

Some of the towns that had depended on the river traffic shrunk to hamlets; others vanished entirely. Following the Second World War, a recreation boom brought new life to the banks of the Grand. The river sprouted cottages and buzzed with motorboats. Parks replaced lock stations, new dams replaced old ones. Today, virtually no trace remains of the original canal.

Yet the banks of the river remain steeped in history, and the roads that follow it are lined with pioneer farms, tall forests and historic hamlets, all providing an unusual backroads drive.

## Brantford to Newport

The first portion of the trip leads to three historic sites and takes you along the high scenic banks of the river. From Highway 2 in Brantford, turn south onto Lock Street and follow the yellow and

blue directional signs to the Mohawk Chapel, about 1.5 km distant. Sitting in a grove of trees that shade an ancient cemetery, this chapel is Ontario's oldest Protestant church and the only Royal Native chapel in the world.

It was on this site that Chief Joseph Brant in 1784 settled his band. They built a school, 24 houses and a small log chapel. The following year they added St. Paul's Chapel, the gleaming white building that you see here. Your next historic site is close at hand, but has a decidedly different story to tell. It is the birthplace of the telephone.

From the Mohawk Chapel, drive left out of the parking lot to Birkett Lane and turn left. Continue for 2 km and turn left again onto Erie Avenue, which becomes County Road 4. After 1 km, you will cross the Grand River and continue to Tutela Heights Road, where you turn right. The yellow and blue signs will direct you to the home of Alexander Graham Bell.

Bell moved here with his parents in 1870 and soon began tinkering with something he called a telephone, an experiment that led to his historic breakthrough in Boston in 1876, when he spoke the first words ever heard through a telephone. It was also from this homestead that, later in 1876, Bell placed the world's first long distance telephone call. It was to Robert White's Boot and Shoe Store in the town of Paris, 14 km away.

The landscaped grounds provide ample parking as well as washrooms, picnic tables, paths for strolling and superb views over the Grand Valley. In the white frame homestead, the rooms are furnished as in Bell's day, and some of his personal effects are on display. Beside the Bell Homestead is the Henderson Building. It was Canada's first telephone exchange and houses a display of interesting and odd early telephones.

The next leg of your journey leads to another historic site with an indigenous theme to it, the birthplace of Canadian poet Pauline Johnson. From the Bell Homestead, return to the intersection of Tutela Heights Road and County Road 4. As you cross the latter, you are on the Newport Road, which lurches down into the valley and follows the river for 2 km to the first of the riverside settlements that you will visit, Newport. The hamlet began life as Burtche's Landing, a shipping point for pine and grain. But as the canal declined so did Newport. Today, the only real vestige is a yellow brick community centre.

From the community centre, turn right and drive the short distance back to County Road 4; turn right and drive to County Road 18, where you turn right again. Cross the bridge and continue to Salt Springs Road and turn right. This quiet country lane wanders along the north bank of the river, past the historic Salt Springs Church and farms that date from the time of the earliest settlements.

After 5 km you will come to a stop sign at Highway 54, known as the Grand River Scenic Parkway. Turn right here, passing through the village of Onondaga, a one-time shipping point on the river. Three km east of Onondaga is Chiefswood, the birthplace of Pauline Johnson. In 1845 Emily Howells, a young English immigrant, met Six Nations chief George Johnson, then a government interpreter. In 1853 they married and Johnson built her this Georgian mansion called Chiefswood, a home that entertained such dignitaries as the Prince of Wales. Their daughter, Pauline Johnson, became an internationally celebrated poet and performer. Today, her birthplace is a museum (open daily in the summer) devoted primarily to Johnson and her works.

Middleport, the next village on your tour, lies a short distance eastward on Highway 54.

**Opposite: Brantford's Royal Mohawk Chapel.**

The board-and-batten church at Middleport dates from the forgotten canal era.

## Middleport

This small and picturesque village began, as the name suggests, as a landing on the Grand River Canal. For a time it shipped timber and grain, and eventually a town plot was laid out. But once canal traffic began to decline, the community dwindled. On the tiny main street, shaded by the trees of the river bank, is an early board-and-batten church. Surrounded by a white picket fence and a spacious cemetery, it dates from the time of the canal.

Opposite: The Grand River near Caledonia.

## Middleport to Caledonia

From Middleport your route continues southeast along Highway 54. In this area, the river's banks recede and become gentle hills, among which are several handsome riverside homes dating back more than a century. After 10 km, you pass under the Highway 6 bridge and enter the town of Caledonia, with its many historic structures. Beneath the railway bridge is the site of one of Caledonia's three canal locks and, opposite the lock, a trio of early canal buildings including the lock master's house and a former hotel.

Few towns of 2,500 can claim as many historic 19th-century buildings as Caledonia. Most of these buildings are within a few blocks of the main intersection. From that intersection go north on Argyle Street to the railway tracks, where the 1904 Grand Trunk railway station has been restored and houses the Chamber of Commerce. The town hall stands two blocks east of the intersection of Argyle and Caithness Streets. This tall brick structure with embedded columns was built in 1857 and has appeared in books featuring Ontario's architectural highlights. With the creation of regional government, the town hall became redundant and is now the Edinburgh Square Heritage and Cultural Centre.

A few paces from the town hall is 46 Caithness Street. This 1847 building was the home of Dr. William McPherson, one of the town's first physicians, and it still retains its second-storey balcony. Dumfries Street runs beside the town hall. Look there for 7 Dumfries, a small frame building covered now with stucco. Originally the Ryan Hotel, it was built in 1854. At 22 Dumfries is a building that once served as a stagecoach inn. Constructed in 1836, it is Caledonia's oldest still-standing building.

The year 1872 marked the coming of the railway, and Caledonia boomed. Many of the buildings in

the downtown core date from those boom years, including the old Opera House. Another, the toll-keeper's house at the eastern end of the bridge, was built in 1857 during a period when toll roads were common, though unpopular.

Before leaving Caledonia, cross the magnificent concrete arch bridge to the south bank, where you will find the oldest mill on the Grand. Built in 1863 on land owned by James Lillie, this four-storey frame gristmill, now restored, has become a popular subject for photographers.

## Caledonia to York

To continue on your route, return from the mill to Argyle Street, and turn right to take you to Haddington Street and there turn left. Haddington becomes River Road and leads past farms that date back more than a century. The road, which follows a high bank about 1 km from the river, offers views of the wide, gentle valley of the Grand. After 6 km, the road comes to an intersection with County Road 9. About 1 km to the left, across the river, lies the sleepy village of York.

Although York is small, it is rich in buildings that date from the canal period. It was located at the site of the second lock on the canal and developed quickly. At its peak it had 450 residents along with several hotels, stores and mills. But when the canal closed and the railways passed York by, its population plummeted to 175 and it became the quiet residential hamlet that you see today.

Cross the bridge and turn right onto Highway 54, which is the main street through the village. Beside the road, at the site of the lock and mill, you will find a small park. Across the road from the park is a red brick structure—a former hotel and just one of the many village buildings that owe their origins to the forgotten canal.

## York to Cayuga

To leave York, continue along Highway 54. After 8 km, you reach a brick gatehouse that marks the entrance to the stunning mansion known as Ruthven Park. This pillared castle, which overlooks the Grand, was built by canal promoter David Thompson in 1845 and contains 36 rooms. A short distance away stood the town of Indiana with its 300 residents and various mills, as well as lock station 1 on the canal. Ruthven remained in the Thompson family until 1994. It was then deeded to the Grand River Land Trust, which has opened it for tours. The furnishings are all original to the Thompson family.

A short drive farther along Highway 54 takes you to Cayuga.

## Cayuga

Another of the canal villages, Cayuga, boomed when the railway reached town, but then it stagnated. Although it was named the county seat in 1850, it remained smaller than its upstream rival, Caledonia, and its current population of 900 is an increase of just 200 over its peak in the 19th century.

As you enter town you pass the courthouse and historic jail beside. Cayuga Street, a once-bustling main street, may be short, but it offers a delightful collection of early brick and stone buildings including a tall, red brick one that housed the post office.

## Cayuga to Port Maitland

To continue to Port Maitland, turn right from the main street onto Highway 3. Drive across the Grand River bridge to the River Road, then turn left. As you cross the bridge you will see off to the right the steel truss railway bridge built by the Canada Southern Railway and now no longer in use.

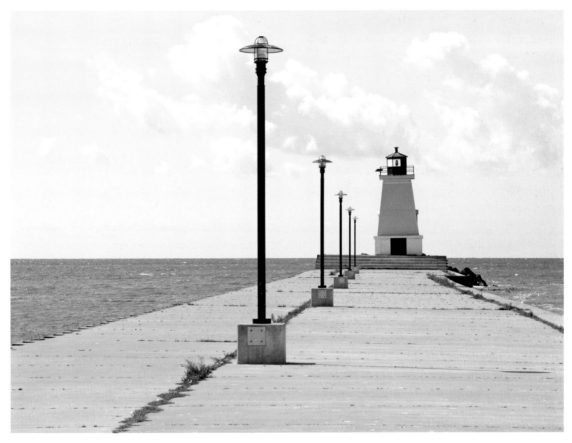

**Port Maitland's historic lighthouse marks the confluence of the Grand River with Lake Erie.**

South of Highway 3, River Road bends east and the river banks disappear as the back shore becomes low, in places swampy. Riverside farms mingle with country homes and rows of cottages. Wide and sluggish, the river is suddenly alive with motorboats and fishermen. After 10 km, the road bends away from the river to Haldimand Road 20. Turn left here. For the last 7 km the land is low, and the views of the river few. A stop sign tells you that you are in a community once known as Byng. Although still known locally as such, its identity has merged with the larger town of Dunnville on the opposite shore of the river. You may wish to visit Dunnville with its busy main street, a riverside park and a variety of fast food restaurants.

From Byng, turn onto County Road 11 and follow it to the mouth of the Grand and the historic port of Port Maitland. More a lake port than a river town, Port Maitland was settled in 1820. Although much is new, you may still see some late 19th-century buildings, including one-time inns, and fishermen's homes along the river. The road ends at the lake. Here, you can park your car and read the historical plaque, which describes the port's early role as a naval depot, or stroll out on the breakwater to the historic Port Maitland lighthouse. You can see by the fishing tugs that Port Maitland retains its link with the past.

# 3 The Face of Farm Country

This backroad leads through Ontario's farming heartland.

This is a route for anyone who is out of touch with their rural roots and craves rolling pastures and "Old Ontario" scenery. The trip starts at Southampton on Lake Huron and follows the fertile farmlands of Bruce and Huron Counties south for 120 km to Bayfield. Along the way, you will encounter some of Ontario's best-preserved 19th-century main streets plus enough farmscapes, riverscapes and old buildings to delight any photographer.

These are not the hobby farms of the wealthy urban commuter, but of those for whom farming is more than a livelihood—it is their life. This area is rural Ontario as it used to be.

There are two chapters to the settlement of Bruce and Huron Counties. The first belongs to energetic land colonizers John Galt and William "Tiger" Dunlop. In 1824 they chartered the Canada Company and advertised extensively in the United Kingdom the bounties of the Huron Tract, the territory that would become Huron County. Most of the land was level and stone-free, and it quickly attracted settlers. By 1850 most of Huron County's farms were taken and the government looked north to Bruce County, then a dark and mysterious forest known as the Queen's Bush.

Farms were surveyed and roads cut through the forest. The first was the Huron Road from Guelph to Goderich on Lake Huron. Then, in 1851, the Elora Road followed, leading from Guelph to Southampton. Before long, the two counties were crisscrossed with a network of farm roads. Villages grew up at important intersections and where the roads crossed water-power sites.

The next chapter belongs to the railways. In 1864 the Wellington, Grey & Bruce Railway began construction from the south, followed by three other lines from the south and east. As usual, towns wily enough to lure the railway burgeoned into important manufacturing centres, while those that were bypassed stagnated. In time even the railways lost their importance. Towns and villages that eventually lost their industries nevertheless continued to serve the farmers, and many retain 19th-century streetscapes of brick stores and shady residential lanes.

## Southampton

The trip starts in the tree-lined streets of Southampton, on Highway 21. Southampton began as a fishing village and became a busy port when the Elora Road was opened in 1851. But its real boomtime began with the completion of the Wellington, Grey & Bruce Railway in 1872 and

Paisley's main street buildings are among Ontario's most historic.

with the growth of several furniture factories. Most of Southampton's buildings date from those years. The main street, only two blocks long, runs west from Highway 21 and ends pleasantly at a long sandy beach. Here, the municipality has developed a small, landscaped rock garden.

On an island about 2 km southwest of the harbour is the Chantry Island lighthouse. This 30 metre stone tower was built in 1859 and is one of the oldest on Lake Huron. The harbour is located a few blocks north of the business district, and here you can launch or rent a boat to visit the historic tower.

On Highway 21, also at the north end of the town, is the museum. Large for a town this size, it contains 11 rooms of artifacts, documents and photographs. Visit the Indian Room, the Fishing Room, and the Pioneer Room. On the grounds

you will find a log cabin and log school, which were brought here from surrounding townships.

At the south end of town, at the corner of Gros-venor and Morpeth Streets, is the attractive brick station built by the Grand Trunk after its takeover of the Wellington, Grey & Bruce Railway. But trains haven't called here for more than 25 years, and the tracks have been lifted. Still, you can almost hear that distant whistle.

## Southampton to Paisley

This portion of your route follows the broad, fertile Saugeen River Valley. Drive out of Southampton south on Highway 21 and turn left onto County Road 3 (the alignment of the old Elora Settlement Road). Three km from the turn, you cross the Saugeen River, where it has carved a rugged gorge into the clay cliffs. (The abandoned iron bridge is worth a look.) The road then bends south and follows a straight course for 14 km. After 2 km you will pass the old road village of Burgoyne, and, after a farther 6 km, the one-time hamlet of Dunblane. Here, set in a grove of willows, is the Dunblane School. It has been altered slightly to become a residence but, with its yellow brick and its bell tower, is one of the most photogenic places on this trip.

Continue for 4 km beyond the school to the turnoff to the Saugeen Bluffs Conservation Area. Its 200 hectares offer camping, fishing, hunting in season and a few short hiking trails. Four km farther on, in a shallow valley where the Teeswater River flows into the Saugeen, is a village in which you will want to linger—the village of Paisley.

## Paisley

Although Paisley dates from 1851, its boom time began 20 years later, with the arrival of the Wellington, Grey & Bruce Railway. By 1890 Paisley had a population of 1,500 and several factories and mills. Today, it claims only two-thirds of that population, while the industries have nearly all vanished.

Thanks to the efforts of interested citizens and a Province of Ontario grant, the main buildings of this attractive village have been preserved and its streets beautified. In the middle of town, on the south side of the bridge, stands the town hall with its delicate bell tower and its sidewalks redone in interlocking brick. Built in 1876, the hall remains the focus of the community. Beside it is the green hose tower of an 1891 fire hall, and across the road looms the 1885 Fisher woollen mill, while on the banks of the river you will see the preserved sawmill. South of the town hall, a string of commercial buildings climb the hillside, most of them dating from 1880–1910.

A short distance west on Mill Drive brings you to Nature's Millworks gift and craft shop, which occupies the five-storey wooden Stark's Mill dating from 1885. Close by is the high-level trestle, which now carries a rail trail high above the river.

## Paisley to Cargill

To leave the village and continue the trip, continue west on Mill Street (County Road 1). The road crosses the bridge and climbs up the wall of the Teeswater River Valley. Stay on this road to where it bends sharply right. At this point you turn left onto Concession Road 20. Drive another 1 km and turn right onto Town Line Road. Here you are on a quiet country road that parallels the busier County Road 3, which lies 2 km to the east. This dirt road is the original alignment of the Elora Settlement Road. That is why the old villages are found on this backroad rather than on the county road.

The road takes you south through Ontario's prime beef country. Green pastures and blowing cornfields are level and stone-free; many of the old wooden barns now sport gleaming aluminum silos. After 6 km, you will meet County Road 15. To follow it on a side trip to the small valley village of Pinkerton, turn right. After 1 km, the road winds into the valley of the Teeswater River and enters Pinkerton, with its feed mill, general store and church.

## Cargill

From Pinkerton, return to the Elora Road, turn right and drive 1.5 km to Cargill. This was until recently a traditional mill town. It dates from 1879, when Henry Cargill bought 1,600 hectares of timber and built a sawmill, a gristmill, a planing mill and a store. Although most of the industries have vanished, the village (population about 100) has retained its collection of yellow brick buildings. As you enter Cargill, turn right onto County Road 32 and cross the bridge. Here you will find the Bailey factory (now abandoned), a brick store that is a block deep, a crescent of identical yellow brick houses, and the Village Inn, located in the old Cargill Hotel.

Return to the Elora Road and turn right. This brings you to a small park where, beside Henry Cargill's millpond, you can picnic or fish.

## Cargill to Formosa

Continue south on Townline Road. For 10 km the road takes you through prosperous farm country. Beef cattle graze lazily on rolling pastures, while in late summer hay and oats waft in the wind. Most farmhouses are large and constructed of yellow or red brick, some elaborately mixing the two colours.

Cross Highway 9 and continue on south. After 1 km, the old Elora Road, here Tower Road, leaves your route and angles southeast. Drive instead straight ahead onto County Road 12, the old Wroxeter Stage Road, which was built to link Wroxeter with the Elora Road.

## Formosa

At 3 km from the intersection, nestled in the wide valley of Formosa Creek, lies the little town of Formosa, settled originally by a colony of Roman Catholic Germans. The location not only spawned the usual mills, but also the trademark of any good German town—a brewery. Formosa's present population of 200 is down from the 350 of its peak years, but it still retains its stores and hotels—and even a descendant of the original brewery.

Although the creek is small, the valley is steep and wide. As you begin your descent, you have a striking view of the village rooftops below. To your left is the Immaculate Conception Church with its soaring steeple—a landmark since 1885. Drive down the hill and follow the main street past the taverns and stores.

## Formosa to Wroxeter

Continue south through the village on County Road 12 as it climbs out of the valley and onto the rolling plain above. At the south end of the village stands the Formosa Springs Brewery. Ontario's traditional small-town beer-making is a tradition that has resurfaced in other small towns across the province. In 1968, this brewery gained national fame as the only such establishment in southern Ontario to defy a long beer strike and stay open. Thirsty customers drove from all parts of central Ontario to line up, some for an entire day, to buy their favourite drink.

For 20 km the road takes you past more fertile farmlands and through forgotten crossroad hamlets with names like Ambleside and Belmore. After crossing Highway 87, you will come to Wroxeter, a "former ghost town" that is coming back to life.

## Wroxeter

Wroxeter dates from 1854, when the Gibson family arrived from Scotland and bought a large tract of land around a water-power site on the Maitland River. Within ten years, Wroxeter had three stores. Twenty years later, when the Toronto, Grey & Bruce Railway arrived, it boomed to five hotels and five blocks of stores, with mills and factories along the Maitland River. But after the turn of the century, Wroxeter's industries began to close. Then, after the First World War, Wroxeter's population began a slow but steady decline and one by one Wroxeter's stores closed. By the late 1940s it had fallen so low that it ceased to be a separate municipality.

Along the wooded river banks, you will find no trace of the old industries that marked Wroxeter's heyday. In the early 1980s Wroxeter's main street resembled that of a ghost town. For three blocks stores sat closed and shuttered. Some have since been demolished, others spruced up to the point

**Brussels' old railway station was saved and moved to a lawn bowling club.**

where a highway sign proudly announces that Wroxeter is now a "Former Ghost Town."

At the south end of the business section, at the corner of Centre and Ann Streets, five roads converge. To continue on your route, cross Ann and then immediately fork right. This will take you through another small neighbourhood and out of the village.

## Wroxeter to Brussels

Drive to the T intersection with County Road 12 and turn left. After 4 km, you will come to Highway 86. Cross it, remaining on County Road 12. Two km from Highway 86 you pass through a nondescript collection of houses known as Jamestown. For the next 8 km you cross farmlands that are flat and so clear of trees that they appear almost prairie-like.

## Brussels

Brussels lies 8 km beyond Jamestown and is another town that shows the scars of decline. It

began in 1852 when William Ainley arrived and laid out a town plot, and William Vanstone erected mills on the Maitland River. In 1864 the rails of the Wellington, Grey & Bruce were laid and turned Brussels into a busy shipping and factory town. The early years of the 20th century were unkind to Brussels, and its population plummeted from 1,800 to today's 1,000. If it weren't for the prosperous farms that surround it yet, it too would have become a ghost town.

Despite the setbacks, Brussels has preserved some of its more important buildings. The bridge over the Maitland River marks the north limit of the business section where the Graham Block is a well-preserved 19th-century commercial building. North of the bridge, the former railway station now sits on the grounds of a lawn bowling club. If you follow the signs from the main street for two blocks to the Brussels Conservation Area, you will see a picturesque Logan gristmill.

The Cardno tower dominates the main street of Seaforth.

## Brussels to Seaforth

Continue south on County Road 12 for 8 km to County Road 25 and the pioneer village of Walton. One of its two original hotels is the handsome red brick Walton Inn Bed and Breakfast. Drive left on County Road 25 for a few metres and then resume your route right onto County Road 12. Once more you pass farmlands that are flat and fertile, and Georgian-style farm homes that were built in the 1840s. Fifteen km from Walton you enter Seaforth, the largest town on this route. Its streetscapes, mansions, and commercial buildings were built in the 19th century, so plan for a prolonged stop here.

Surprisingly, Seaforth is younger than its two suburbs, Egmondville and Harpurhey. Named for Constant Van Egmond, one of the builders of the Huron Road (Highway 8), Egmondville sits on the banks of Silver Creek, 2 km south of the heart of

town. The place became a busy village with taverns, shops, three stores and Van Egmond's sawmill and gristmill. In 1839, 3 km northwest of Egmondville, on the Huron Road, landowner Dr. William Chalk opened a post office and surveyed a townsite. With traffic on the Huron Road heavy, the site was ideal for a village. Harpurhey, as he called it, soon contained two hotels and three blacksmith shops, plus a store and several other shops. Meanwhile, the intersection of the Bayfield Road (as County Road 12 was called then) and the Huron Road itself, where Seaforth would later grow, remained a swamp.

When the railway arrived in Brussels and the Bayfield Road was extended to it, the intersection sprang to life. It boomed even more when in 1870 it got a railway of its own. By 1900 Seaforth's population had soared to 2,500 and overshadowed its pioneer predecessors. Although most of the town's early factories have long since gone, Seaforth remains a major regional shopping town. Its commercial core extends about four blocks and is one of western Ontario's most striking.

Guarding the main street like sentries are three towers. On the east are the towers of the town hall (built in 1893) and the post office. On the west side is the tower of the Cardno Opera House, built in 1877. On the back streets are several 19th-century mansions, such as 99 Goderich Street West, built within the first half-decade of Seaforth's existence; 38 Louisa Street, at John, another of Seaforth's oldest homes; and 88 Goderich Street East, which dates from the 1860s and was built by Dr. T. Coleman, the village's first reeve.

Seaforth's most historic building can be seen on your way out of town. Drive south on Main Street, and after 1.5 km, you will come to the brick mansion that Constant Van Egmond built in 1846. Preserved and restored by the Van Egmond Foundation, it is open to the public during the summer.

South of it, County Road 3 (the old Bayfield Road) forks from County Road 12 and leads west toward the Lake Huron port of Bayfield, the oldest village on this trip, and the last.

Side Trip: From Seaforth, follow Highway 8 west to Clinton and then Highway 4 south to the signs for the "Clinton School Car." This refurbished passenger coach is that last surviving school car which brought education to the isolated railway communities in northern Ontario between 1928 and 1966.

## Seaforth to Bayfield

Follow County Road 3 for 8 km across Huron County's flat clay plains. A stop sign marks Highway 4, and here you pass through the tiny village of Brucefield. Sadly, insensitive highway widening has removed many of Brucefield's early crossroads buildings. After a farther 6 km on County Road 3 you will come to another small crossroads hamlet, Varna. Here, an old general store and feed mill hug the intersection and carry on the hamlet's traditional role as a farm service village. A further 9 km brings you to the end of your trip, and to the remarkable village of Bayfield.

## Bayfield

Through a gap in the high clay bluffs, the Bayfield River swirls into Lake Huron and forms a small but protected harbour. Bayfield is remarkable in many ways. It is one of Lake Huron's earliest communities, its streets radiate from a central park, and its tree-lined main street is one of the best preserved in the province.

Many Ontario villages were raw forest in 1836, when Bayfield was already a busy port, and settlers departed daily along the Bayfield Road to their lands in the interior. But the railways went elsewhere and, by the end of the century, Bayfield was in decline. Although a small fishing fleet and the productive farmlands of Bayfield's hinterland prevented it from becoming a ghost town, it was only when Lake Huron's shore became a popular recreation mecca that the town revived.

On Bayfield's outskirts, County Road 3 ends at Highway 21. Turn right here and drive 1 km to Clan Gregor Park, the main square where the streets converge. Turn left at the park and follow its perimeter to Main Street.

Bayfield is best enjoyed on foot. Its main street is a wide avenue two blocks long, where the stores and businesses occupy separate buildings cooled by large shade trees. As you walk north from the park the first building on the left is the Albion Hotel, which was built in 1840 and still provides food and drink. Across from the hotel, on the east side, is a trio of early buildings, including the Village Store (now a hair salon) and the Rogers

Bayfield's strollable main street.

House, built in 1834 and one of the town's oldest structures.

The Little Inn, built in 1847 and the street's most prominent structure, is surmounted by a cupola. Its wraparound porch has recently been reconstructed. Inside, the rooms have been refurbished in the style of the 19th century, including the licensed dining room.

From the north end of Louisa Street, Long Hill Road winds down the wall of the steep ravine that forms the harbour. At the end of the street are a parking lot and the beach. Although the beach is stony, it offers a pleasant view south along the steep shore bluffs of Lake Huron. At the marina the slender masts of the pleasure craft form a thick forest, while on the opposite side of the harbour

you may see the few remaining tugs of the Bayfield fishing fleet. From the bluff atop the west end of Bayfield Terrace, enjoy the spectacular sunsets for which Lake Huron is famous.

If you are returning to central or eastern Ontario, retrace your steps to Seaforth and follow Highway 8 east, leading you to Kitchener and Highway 401. To reach the London area, return on County Road 3 to Brucefield and take Highway 4 south. For the Windsor area, take Highway 21 south from Bayfield.

Opposite: The Lake Huron shoreline at Bayfield.

# 4 The Bruce Peninsula Road

Winding beneath brooding limestone cliffs and past the remains of pioneer farms and lumber camps, this backroad probes what is probably Ontario's best-known backwater, the Bruce Peninsula. Starting in the town of Owen Sound, on Provincial Highway 10, it twists and bumps along 130 km of quiet old farm roads, climbing up the east side of the Bruce Peninsula and ending at a remote point of rock called Cabot Head.

If you are coming from Toronto, Kitchener or farther away, you may wish to consider spending the night. Owen Sound abounds in good motels and campgrounds, though there are few at the other end of the route. Wherever you stay, reserve ahead. During the summer, the morning ferry to Manitoulin Island from Tobermory is so popular that motels are usually full.

A long limestone finger, the Bruce Peninsula divides Lake Huron from Georgian Bay. On its eastern side, the high cliffs of the Niagara Escarpment plunge into Georgian Bay's clear waters. The west side of the peninsula is a marked contrast. Amid a shoreline of swampy coves, the limestone plain slips quietly beneath Lake Huron.

This is a trip for every outdoors person. For spelunkers and geologists, there are caves and the strange rock pillars known as flowerpots. Plant lovers can rummage around the swamps for the rare calypso orchid and other unusual flowers and plants, while hikers can clamber over some of the roughest portions of the famous Bruce Trail. And for divers, there is Ontario's only underwater park, Fathom Five National Marine Park, with its treasure trove of wrecks.

A typical waterfall along the Niagara Escarpment.

ettlement on the Bruce has always been sparse. Archaeologists claim that, despite a few small fur posts, the Native population was light. When the townships of the Bruce were surveyed into farm lots in the 1850s, the few settlers were more interested in selling the timber than in farming.

Sawmilling was the primary industry of the peninsula throughout its early years. At one time or another, most of the protected west coast coves housed a mill and a small community, but there were few settlements on the exposed shoreline of the east coast. Inland from the coasts, the bedrock and boulders discouraged the few pioneer farming communities that did start up, and today only two remain.

Tourists have now replaced the farmers and lumbermen; and campers, hikers, divers, nature lovers and cottagers flock to the peninsula.

## Owen Sound to Wiarton

Owen Sound sits at the head of a deep bay bordered by the cliffs of the Niagara Escarpment. It contains a full range of shops, most of them downtown, on or near 16th Street, the street that the highway follows. Begin the route at a fitting site, the Marine Rail Heritage Centre on 3rd Avenue West, which is housed in a preserved CNR railway station on the west side of the harbour. Drive north on 3rd Avenue until it becomes County Road 1 and follows the shoreline of the bay.

At 6 km from the downtown core is the Indian Falls Conservation Area. In late spring and early summer, Indian Creek falls veil-like into a 20 metre gorge. An easy 1 km wooded walking trail follows the gorge to the falls. Unfortunately, unless the weather has been rainy, the river is usually dry by midsummer.

North of the falls, the route passes farms and pastures. Small hamlets, which once catered to the needs of the local farmers, cluster about most crossroads. East Linton, 3 km from the park, still has its landmark, the 100-year-old brick United church just west of the intersection. Some 4 km farther on, at the next crossroads, the hamlet of Hogg contains a one-room schoolhouse, now a private residence. Here County Road 1 goes right, but instead you should continue north on Kemble Rock Road. Another 5 km bring you to the larger crossroads village of Kemble, where the brick Methodist church is now a senior citizens' home.

In this area, the escarpment lies about 4 km from the water's edge. The road itself is about 1 km from the water, and the plain between is a fertile and prosperous farming area. From Kemble, drive north. After 2 km the road grinds up a wooded outlier of the Niagara Escarpment, where, to the right, the view extends across the waters of Owen Sound Bay. Continue 2 km, follow the road left for another 1 km, and turn right at Big Bay Road.

The view that greets you is sudden and panoramic. Here, at the brink of the cliffs, the ground drops to a flat pastoral plain that stretches 2 km to the blue waters of Colpoys Bay and its green, wooded islands. Extending out of sight on the horizon is the long, white cliff line of the Bruce Peninsula.

Drive down the hill and across the plain. On the shoreline sits the hamlet of North Keppel, shown on today's maps as "Big Bay." A former shipping village, it still contains a general store and several original houses. Here you rejoin County Road 1. Turn left and follow the shore road for 5 km. This road skirts the water, squeezing a string of cottages against the shore. Then, as the road swings inland, it climbs a shore cliff. Continue for a few metres and look for a small park and lookout, the Colpoy Lookout, where you can pause and enjoy the view across Colpoys Bay or have a picnic. Here, the escarpment consists of two bluffs—the 50 metre

Owen Sound's Grand Trunk station is preserved as a museum.

shore cliff in front of you and, behind you, Skinner Bluff. On the narrow plain, early settlers tried to farm. But the soil was shallow and rocky, and most farms failed. As you follow the plain, you can see the remains of these farms, though many of the houses are more modern.

Another 4 km from the little park, the road eases inland and up the second cliff to a yawning limestone cave. At the brow of the hill, watch for the sign to Bruce's Cave Conservation Area. There is neither a gate fee nor any facilities. But from the dirt parking lot you can follow the trail through the woods for half a kilometre to the cave. It has no passages but is a deep ballroom-like cavern in the rock wall, its opening divided by a high rock pillar. A second, smaller cave lies a few metres away.

From the conservation area, resume your route along County Road 1. After 1 km, you will cross

Wiarton's Grand Trunk station has been moved to a waterside campground.

a small bridge over a tumbling stream and enter the hamlet of Oxenden. There are two buildings of historic note here. One lies beside the stream and is the gristmill, built in 1866, when Oxenden was a busy landing and farm-service village. The mill is now covered with stucco and has been converted to a private dwelling. The other building of note is the village store at the northwest corner of the intersection. Although the store is no longer in business, it retains many of the century-old architectural features that typified the general store of a century ago.

Your next stop, Wiarton, lies 3 km farther along.

## Wiarton

Wiarton offers a combination of heritage buildings and waterside recreation. Located at the head of Colpoys Bay and nestled beneath the cliffs of the escarpment, the town is a relative latecomer to southern Ontario's urban scene. It began around 1870 with the lucrative trade in lumber, and only ten years later had eight sawmills. When the railway arrived, not only did the fishing industry boom, but furniture factories became Wiarton's main industry. Meanwhile, the town's population swelled to more than 2,000. Today, sleek yachts have replaced the fishing tugs, and a campground and park have replaced the factories.

The road from Oxenden enters Wiarton from the east on Frank Street. Follow it to Highway 6 (Berford Street) and turn right. This is the main street and it takes you to the commercial core, where you will find a few small restaurants. If you need to replenish your picnic supplies, there are grocery and variety stores.

There are a few historic buildings in Wiarton

that are worth a look. Among these are the two former hotels in the downtown area, which were built before the turn of the century. One is near William Street and the other at Boyd. Farther north, the three-storey stone feed mill, which supplied local farmers since 1903, has been renovated for commercial uses. At the campground, Bluewater Park, lies one of the town's most important heritage buildings, its 1904 railway station.

If you turn right past the feed mill and follow Division Street to its end, you come to the yacht basin and Wiarton's restored waterfront.

Leave Wiarton north on Highway 6 and take a detour into the Spirit Rock Conservation Area to see the shell of the "castle" Corran, home of Member of Parliament Alexander McNeill from 1881 to 1901. After 3 km, turn right onto County Road 9. This road soon descends the escarpment to the shore and enters the village of Colpoys Bay, an early sawmill village that predates Wiarton by two decades.

From Colpoys Bay, the route follows a network of pioneer concession roads that crisscross the flat, table-like top of the escarpment. Sometimes they swoop down to hug the shore; other times, they soar to the brink of the cliff, providing views of distant headlands and sparkling bays. Short side trips lead to caves, coves and quiet beaches.

Stay on County Road 9 as it swings inland from Colpoys Bay. Drive north for 4 km and then turn right onto County Road 18. Continue for 5 km through a few pockets of pastureland to Purple Valley Road and turn left. Here, you will come upon a small collection of buildings in the colourfully named Purple Valley, an important centre for early pioneers.

Continue north for another 5 km. The second road right from Purple Valley, McIver Road, leads to the Cape Croker Indian Reserve. With its campgrounds, village, historic lighthouse and one of the peninsula's oldest churches, it makes an interesting side trip.

To continue on your route, carry on north from McIver Road. The road bends left and soon reconnects with County Road 9. Turn right to Hope Bay. The side road from County Road 9 to Hope Bay is only 1 km long, but as it descends the escarpment it provides you with a picturesque vista over the bay, walled on both sides by limestone bluffs. A century ago, Hope Bay was a busy shipping centre for lumber, but today cottages have replaced the workers' homes on the narrow streets, and a public beach and campground have replaced the docks and the wood piles. At the beach, you can stretch your legs and have a picnic before resuming your trip.

## Hope Bay to Lion's Head

From Hope Bay, continue north on County Road 9. This road, which runs as straight as the terrain permits, was surveyed as a farm road, part of a system of concession roads that enabled settlers to travel to their farm lots. But in this area, as through much of the Bruce, the soils were rocky and the farms short-lived. You will pass fields that are overgrown—many reclaimed entirely by the forest—and the gaunt shells of cabins and barns that peer from the bush.

About 4 km from the Hope Bay turnoff, watch for signs pointing to the Greig's Caves. A road on the right leads you 3 km to the site. The caves are a popular attraction on private property, and there is a charge for a tour. These caves were home to prehistoric cave dwellers in the movie *Quest for Fire*. Shortly after the movie was filmed, one unsuspecting stroller discovered, to his horror, a fur-clad body lying on the ground. Not until he learned that it was a discarded dummy used during a fight scene in the movie did he breathe a heavy sigh of relief.

From the Greig's Caves turnoff, County Road 9 twists northward through a rocky woodland for 2 km and suddenly emerges onto a wide plain. Originally a swamp, the Eastnor Plain was drained to produce the most prosperous farming community on the peninsula. It is now a treeless landscape of green fields, grazing cattle and blowing hay.

Most large farming areas have their mill towns, and here that is Barrow Bay. After travelling 1 km over the plain and across a bridge, you will see a pair of unusual old buildings on the left side of the road. The first one, a simple board-and-batten affair, is the former office of the Barrow Bay Lumber Company, and it dates back more than 100 years. Beside it is a general store. If you look downstream from the bridge, you will see a stone wall. This is all that remains of Barrow Bay's mill dam. The foundations of the mill (which burned in 1947) now support a modern cottage.

Continue north across the plain for a farther 4 km and you will come to Lion's Head, the largest town north of Wiarton on the peninsula.

## Lion's Head

This town of 600, located on a small sheltered harbour, began as a centre for shipping and fishing. The prosperity of the farming community elevated it to a busy commercial centre at the turn of the century, and tourism has helped to keep it that way.

You enter the town on the main street, where there are shops, motels, restaurants and a bank. The municipal beach offers camping, picnicking, bathing and access to the Bruce Trail. Extending into the harbour is a long public wharf, from which you can see everything from luxury yachts to simple runabouts. Looming over the harbour, the great wall of the Niagara Escarpment reaches out to a craggy headland. Before it eroded, the rocky profile resembled the head of a lion, the feature that gave the village its name.

**The historic Cabot Head lighthouse is now a museum.**

## Lion's Head to Cabot Head

This last section of the route traces little-used concession roads through some of the emptiest parts of the peninsula and then follows a rocky shoreline beneath looming limestone cliffs to a remote headland.

Leave Lion's Head by driving north on the main street, which before long swerves down to the water and to the wide expanse of Whippoorwill Bay. During the next 2 km, after passing a string of cottages, you will find several opportunities to pull over to the roadside. Wander along the rocky shore or cast a line into the surf. From the northern head of the bay, the road bends inland where you follow the Forty Hills Road north. This rugged limestone ridge continues to defy road-building and forces the gravel road to snake precariously around each outcropping. The bends are sharp, so look out for oncoming traffic.

After 3 km, the road emerges from the hills into the one-time farming community of Cape Chin.

Most of the farms have been abandoned, leaving behind the ruins of their log cabins.

At the next intersection, continue straight ahead and, a kilometre later, look for a stone church standing alone in an empty field. This is the widely known and much-photographed St. Margaret's Chapel, which was completed in 1930. It took three years to finish and was a community effort. The area's determined farmers hauled stone from the fields and little quarries to erect the solid church. The stained-glass windows were donated by a factory in London, Ontario, and the oak pews from a local parishioner. The bell came from a Canadian Northern Railway steam locomotive.

North of the church, the road bends sharply right. Keep left on East Road. For the next 9 km, follow another old concession road through swamps and around rock outcrops. A few pioneers tried to carve out farms here, but the overgrown fields and derelict barns testify to the futility of their efforts. After 10 km, the road ends abruptly at a T intersection at Brinkman's Corners with the Dyers Bay Road. Turn right and travel 4 km to another T intersection. Turn right again and descend the hill into the little waterside village of Dyers Bay—and to a vista that you will be unlikely to forget.

Once a thriving lumber town, Dyers Bay now consists of a store, a restaurant and a string of cottages. Here you start the last and most scenic portion of the route. From the village, the road winds along the narrow beach 10 km to Cabot Head. After 3 km the cottages begin to thin out, until there is just no more room at the base of the huge cliff.

Roughly 2.5 km from the last cottage, the road crosses a small culvert. If you are a hiker, stop here and explore the remains of one of Ontario's more ingenious sawmill efforts. In 1881, Horace and Robert Lymburner acquired rights to the timber that covered the mesa atop the bluffs. There, Gillies Lake empties down a cascading stream into Georgian Bay, 100 metres below. Down on the beach, where tugs could haul the lumber off to the south shore and the railways, the Lymburners built a mill and a town. At first the logs were simply hurled down the cliff into a small pond on the beach. But the damage to the logs was so enormous that the Lymburners decided to build a log slide. By damming the outlet from Gillies Lake and periodically allowing great gushes of water and rock to plummet down the steep gully, erosion soon carved a natural flume, which was then lined with planks. But by 1905 the timber was gone and the Lymburner mill fell silent.

From the mill site, a drive of 5 km brings you to Cabot Head, one of the most placid points of land in Ontario. Here, at the northeasterly point of the peninsula, a lonely lighthouse is the sole remaining building of what was once a bustling sawmilling and fishing village. Dating from 1896, the restored wooden light tower and keeper's dwelling is now a museum. Here, too, you will find Wingfield Basin, a former port but now a wildlife area with a boardwalk and the hull of a wrecked ship.

This is the end of the road. Here, the escarpment changes direction and runs westward in a wild, rocky and unsettled shoreline. By following Dyers Bay Road back out to Highway 6, you can drive north to Tobermory, home of the *MS Chi-Cheemaun* (the car ferry to Manitoulin Island), boat tours to remarkable Flowerpot Island, and Fathom Five National Marine Park. Highway 6 south returns you to Wiarton.

**Opposite: Flowerpot Island.**

# 5 Cuestas and Valleys

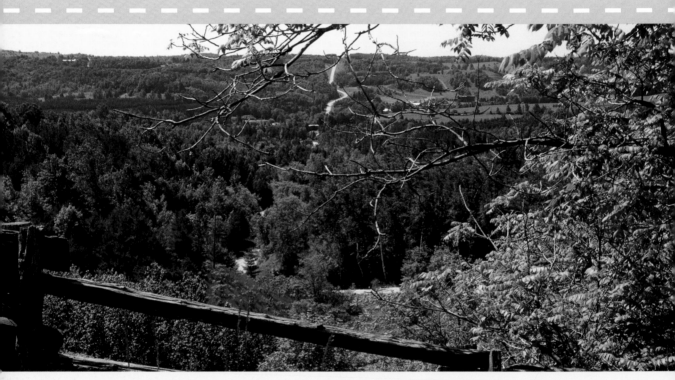

The Hockley Valley is one of many beautiful valleys in this region.

This route guides you through the valleys and to breathtaking vistas of Ontario's most unusual and scenic geological feature, the Niagara Escarpment. The route begins at Orangeville, 60 km northwest of Toronto, and for 80 km it follows backroads northward over old concession roads, plunges into wide valleys and soars onto rocky cuestas. (A cuesta is a long, low ridge with a gentle slope on one side and a steep cliff on the other.) It ends in the Beaver Valley, one of the province's most beautiful valleys.

With its windswept lookouts, pastoral lowlands and tumbling streams, this trail will appeal to the recreational driver. The hiker can gain access to the Bruce Trail at several points, and the aficionado of Ontario's rural vernacular architecture will discover outstanding 19th-century farm homes, churches, schools and even Orange lodges.

The villages along the route are small and few contain gas stations or restaurants, so you would be advised to stock up at Orangeville before starting out.

the scene of the zany River Rat Race. Each spring a flotilla of offbeat craft (anything but boats are allowed) bounce their way downstream, their navigators outlandishly attired.

The valley narrows here and its walls steepen to form a gorge and to provide some of Ontario's more popular ski slopes. In the valley bottom, County Road 7 stops at County Road 13. Here, a high, rocky cliff known locally as Mount Baldy looms above you. Turn right onto County Road 13 and you will shortly enter the former mill village of Kimberley, which still has many of its historic buildings and now caters to skiers. Even the old board-and-batten mill has become an antique shop.

Drive south from Kimberley on County Road 13. As the road climbs back up the east wall, the valley narrows until it is only 1 km wide, its walls almost sheer. After 2 km, a small viewpoint on the right offers you a last view down the valley before you leave it.

## Eugenia Falls

About 6 km from Kimberley you enter the hamlet of Eugenia Falls, where small signs direct you to the Eugenia Falls Conservation Area. Here, again,

the local conservation authority has been at work. Covering 23 hectares, this wooded park offers picnicking, hiking and a view of the 30-metre-high Eugenia Falls. You can see the gorge carved by the creek, and, on the opposite bank above the falls, a strange-looking limestone arch looking out of place in the hillside. This is the vestige of a failed attempt to create a power dam; the arch was to be the entrance to the underground flume. The gorge was the site of a "gold" rush in the 1850s, which prompted surveyors to lay out an extensive network of streets, anticipating a golden boomtown. But the "gold" turned out to be nothing more than iron pyrite, or "fool's gold," and the streets remained largely undeveloped. Now the lots are sprouting newer country homes.

This is a fitting place to end your tour of the escarpment, a location where one of the cuesta's features has been preserved for the public. It lends hope that this unique and attractive prehistoric ridge can be preserved for future generations and protected from insensitive development.

About 4 km from Eugenia Falls, County Road 13 ends at County Road 4, from which point Flesherton on Highway 10 lies about 4 km west.

N

Lake
Ontario

Bay of
Quinte

Long
Point

Milford

Picton

Demorestville

Northport

Belleville

Rednersville

10

Trenton

33

401

62

28

45

Rice
Lake

Harwood

Gores
Landing

Bewdley

18

Garden
Hill

Cobourg

Peterborough

115

Elizabethville

9

Kirby

Burketon

Tyrone

Oshawa

7

8

Raglan

47

Claremont

1

48

Aurora

11

Lake
Simcoe

Shanty Bay

Coulson

6

Orillia

Vasey

Barrie

400

407

Toronto

Brampton

401

10

Mississauga

Caledon East

7

Palgrave

400

Penetanguishene

Victoria
Harbour

Waubaushene

Port McNicoll

12

11

400

# Section 2
# Central Ontario

# 6 Those Surprising Simcoe County Highlands

**Carley Station was once a busy station village on the Canadian Pacific Railway.**

Next time you venture north to Muskoka's cottage country, try and spend some time exploring the little-known yet often spectacular hill country of Simcoe County. This trip starts in the historic waterside mill town of Waubaushene on Highway 12 and zigzags south over 70 km of gravel concession roads through Simcoe's hills. Many of the views along the route are just as spectacular as those of the more famous Ottawa Valley or the Niagara Escarpment.

Summer offers bass and trout fishing in Georgian Bay at the north end of the route and in Lake Simcoe at the south end. The fall season brings out some of Ontario's best colours in the maple forests that shelter the winding roads. For admirers of country architecture, there are farmhouses of stone, brick and wood. And the forests and closed concession roads offer ideal hiking and skiing trails.

Simcoe County's first roads were military. During the War of 1812, two supply roads were built to move troops and equipment to the forts that guarded northern Lake Huron. The first was the Nine Mile Portage, a wagon road that linked Lake Simcoe with Willow Creek, a tributary flowing to Georgian Bay. The second was the Penetanguishene Road, which barged straight northward from a townsite called Kempenfeldt, also on Lake Simcoe, to the garrisons at Penetanguishene on Georgian Bay. Today the Penetanguishene Road has become Highway 93, and the Nine Mile Portage has vanished.

Following the War of 1812, the Penetanguishene Road was surveyed into farm lots, which were offered free to half-pay veterans of the war. After 1830, more settlers arrived to take up land in the back townships. A mixed group, they included Germans, Irish, Scots and fugitive American slaves, whose simple frame church still stands. Then, during the 1850s and 1860s, railways pierced the area and brought a new wave of growth, especially to the little ports that ringed the bay. A half-dozen ports soon boomed into busy sawmill towns. But when the roar of the mills and the puffing of the trains faded, so did most of the towns. Meanwhile, on the hillsides, many farmers found the steep, stony lands awkward and unproductive, and they moved away. In recent years, both areas have revived through tourism—the mill towns because of the popularity of Georgian Bay's waters and shores, and the hills for downhill skiing.

## Waubaushene to Victoria Harbour

Beside the turnoff from Highway 400 onto Highway 12 sits what in 1860 was the largest of the mill towns, Waubaushene. Its industries and businesses, and many of its workers' cabins, have now vanished, and several new homes can be seen on the network of streets that overlook Georgian Bay.

But a few reminders of the mill days linger on.

If you wish to look around Waubaushene, turn right at the directional arrow on Highway 12 and follow Pine Street up the hill. At the crest was once the commercial core, where Waubaushene Heritage and Maddison's Garden Centre occupy early buildings. As you continue along Pine Street, the red brick St. John's Roman Catholic Church comes into view. Continue down the hill to Hazel Street and turn right. On your left are Georgian Bay's waters and the board-and-batten gothic Memorial Church with its slender white steeple. The road bends to the right, where Government Dock Road leads to the shoreline before curving back to the Coldwater Road. Turn left here and you will find access to the Tay Shore Trail, which follows the scenic shoreline almost into Midland.

To continue your trip, follow Highway 12 for 8 km west of Waubaushene and look for the directions into the village of Victoria Harbour. To reach the historic centre, follow Park Street to Richard Street and keep left to Albert Street, where you turn right to reach William Street. This intersection marks the main part of town. To the north, newer development marks the harbour—once the site of the busy King and Fowlie mills.

Although the place is much smaller than it was then, it has retained many early features. Several of the commercial buildings and the post office at the main intersection date from the milling era. Look particularly at the facade of the restored wooden building on the northwest corner. Extending west on William Street for more than 2 km are similar two-storey houses once occupied by the mill workers. Most of these buildings have been renovated or are hidden beneath layers of aluminum siding.

## Victoria Harbour to Vasey

William Street rejoins Highway 12. Follow the highway west to Triple Bay Road and drive to Port McNicoll and the new home of the historic CPR steamship the *SS Keewatin*. The 1907 vessel, now a museum, is the focus of a shoreline development that will include reminders from the port's railway and steamship era. From Port McNicoll return to Highway 12. Go back east to Reeves Road (Tay Concession 5) and turn right. After 1.5 km you will see a historical marker pointing left down a side road to the site of St. Louis. Near this spot in 1649, the invading Iroquois tortured to death two Jesuits, Jean de Brébeuf, and Gabriel Lalemant. The Iroquois went on to sweep the Hurons and the Jesuits from Simcoe County and to become kings of the fur trade. This site, open only during the summer, is a memorial to the Jesuit martyrs.

Continue south on Reeves Road and be sure to keep your camera handy, for here the road climbs out of the valley of Hogg Creek and onto a high ridge. As you reach the summit, turn right onto Hogg Valley Road. After 1 km this road takes you back to the crest, and suddenly a vista of pastoral serenity unfolds at your feet, revealing in the flat valley a quiltwork of traditional farms.

Considering the size of the valley, the creek that meanders across its floor is surprisingly small. Most geologists believe that this little stream did not carve the valley by itself, but, rather, that it flows through a wide swath gouged out of the earth by glacial meltwaters 30,000 years ago. Because the valley runs at a 45-degree angle to the grid pattern of the roads, you must make one more zig into the valley before you zag back out of it. As you descend the hill, note the foundations of the barn on the right. You may at first think that these are stones, but look closer: they were the ends of logs used in an early construction method known as "stacklog."

Turn left onto Rumney Road, Concession 4, as soon as you reach the bottom of the valley, and grind up another steep grade for more than 1 km.

Travel on to the next intersection with the 7th Line and turn left. After 2 km, look for Mill Pond Road and turn right. This road leads into another of those little gulches that cross the valley floor. This one, however, had enough water power to fuel the little mill village of Coulson. It is still a pretty spot, and a few of the old village residences have been converted to modern houses. The road winds on through pasture lands, ending at Medonte Concession Road 6 (Line 6), where steep wooded slopes loom on the left. These are the foothills of the great Sand Hills. Turn left and continue until you come to County Road 22.

## The Sand Hills

The Sand Hills were formed during the last ice age, when the retreating ice sheets halted and the raging meltwaters pushed sand, stones and boulders into great mounds. On this rugged ridge, early settlers purchased farm lots sight unseen. It was a decision most regretted, for the hills proved too steep and the sands too dry and bouldery for even the crudest farming. Most settlers left in disgust, and today the Sand Hills have reverted to forest.

Concession Road 6 ends at County Road 22. Turn right here and follow this paved road for 1 km to Oro Concession Road 5. Then turn left. This rugged road is not maintained and should be avoided during winter and early spring. In the heart of the Sand Hills, the forests part at intervals to reveal abandoned fields and overgrown foundations—reminders of the backbreaking attempts to wrest crops from this unyielding area. (If Concession 5 is unusable, go to Concession 4, farther west, as an alternative.)

After 3 km, the road intersects the Bass Lake Road. Turn left. This road is maintained and is passable year-round. It also marks the most rugged section of the trip. As it winds through a forest of pine and maple, it occasionally passes former pastures, long abandoned and overgrown. After 6 km, follow Oro 8th Line to the right for a few metres and then turn left to resume the Bass Lake Road. For the next 2.5 km the Sand Hills loom to the right. Below you on the left the fringe of productive farmland encroaches. Beyond lie the distant waters of Bass Lake. Although the lake is small and is becoming polluted, it remains popular with campers and cottagers.

At the next crossroads, that with the Oro 10th Line, turn right. This road takes you directly across the Sand Hills at one of their highest points. Here, the road climbs a steep, wooded gully and passes a couple of farms that have struggled to survive on one of the few pockets of better soil. Although the ridge is 20 km long, it varies only from 1 km to 2 km in width. By the time you reach the next intersection, the Rugby Road, you will be on the south slope of the ridge. Stretching before you and on to Lake Simcoe 8 km to the south, the terrain is flat and the farms productive. Your trip ends where the 10th Line reaches Highway 11. You may turn right only at this point to head west.

If you still have time, you can continue south from Highway 11 to County Road 20, Ridge Road, named for a ridge that was a lakeshore bluff from an earlier and higher Lake Simcoe. This is a former pioneer trail, now lined with country homes, and is an attractive way to finish your trip into Barrie. Be sure to pause in Shanty Bay to see St. Thomas Church, built in 1838 using mud.

# 7 The Ridge Road West

Within the shadow of Toronto's skyscrapers there is a series of roads that wind along a ridge of billowing fields, through hardwood forests and past stone houses and churches that date back more than a century and a half. Here is a country landscape that has still mostly defied the sprawl of look-alike houses and fast-food drive-ins that mark the Greater Toronto Area's urban fringe.

The route starts at the intersection of Yonge Street and Bloomington Road, 2 km south of Aurora and about 30 km north of downtown Toronto. It zigzags westward along a series of country roads for about 50 km and ends at Highway 10 just 20 km south of Orangeville.

**The views extend in several directions from Mount Wolfe.**

Most of the land along it is private, and the opportunities to hike or picnic are few. Snack bars, grocery stores and gas stations are located along the main cross streets, such as Yonge Street, Airport Road and Highway 10.

N ext to the Niagara Escarpment, central Ontario's most prominent landscape feature is the great Oak Ridges Moraine. About 20,000 years ago the waters from melting glaciers carried sand, gravel, boulders and even great chunks of the glacier itself into a long fissure in the ice, creating this ridge of rugged hills that stretches from Orangeville to Trenton.

Between the ridge and the lake lies a level clay plain that has provided some of the best farmland in Canada. Here, early settlers cleared their farms, gradually extending northward from Lake Ontario until they struck the great Oak Ridge. Its steep hills defied road-building, and only a few winding trails penetrated low saddles in the hills. Not until the 1830s did the pioneers penetrate the ridge. At first the tall pines gave rise to a prosperous sawmill industry. But because the high country cradled the headwaters of the rivers that flow into Lake Ontario, the streams were small and mill sites few. As a result, the villages were scattered and served only the immediate needs of the pioneers. Moreover, farming was poor. Boulders and stones plagued the steep hillsides, and the sandy subsoils retained little water. Many of the farmers left, weary and defeated.

During the 1930s, under a system of county forests managed by the Ontario government, the worst lands were replanted in pine. Later, during the 1960s and 1970s, much of the remaining land was sold to developers or to wealthy commuters. Nevertheless, the area retains a landscape of spacious grasslands, dark forests and spectacular views.

## Aurora to Eversley

Follow Yonge Street north from Toronto, or take Bloomington Road west from Highway 404 to the intersection with Yonge Street. Continue west from Yonge Street. At the southwest corner of

Bathurst Street, 2 km west, stands a large fieldstone farmhouse. It hugs the roadside and dates back to the earliest days of settlement. Thoughtful owners have preserved it in its original condition.

Continue west for a further 2 km and you will come to Eversley and its old stone church. Begun in 1834 as a crossroads hamlet, Eversley takes its name from a village in Hampshire, England. On the northeast corner of the intersection is the one-time general store, now a private residence. The blacksmith's shop, which stood on the southeast corner, has long vanished. However, just 0.7 km south stands the most remarkable building on this route, the Eversley Church.

Early pioneers yearned for a place to worship. They gathered up the stones from their fields and laid them together to build the Eversley Presbyterian Church. The year was 1838. Services were held there until 1958, when the stone church was closed. Concern over whether this handsome structure would survive was lifted in 1960 when Lady Eaton, who had owned a large estate to the north, purchased the building so that it could be preserved. It stands today amid its pioneer headstones, with a plaque in front to recount its story.

## Eversley to Kettleby

Near Eversley, two kettle lakes appear on two large estates, both of which are open to the public. Geologists will tell you that a kettle lake is a pond in a depression that formed during the glacial retreat when a huge chunk of ice was trapped in the sands of the ridge and gradually melted to leave a large hole.

The first of these lakes is at Eaton Hall. From the Eversley Church, drive north 2 km, turn left into the grounds of Seneca College, King Campus, and follow the lane to the right, leading you to Eaton Hall. Built in 1919 by Sir John Eaton of department store fame, this estate was a popular summer

retreat for the Eaton family. The last to use it was Lady Eaton. On her death in 1971 it became the property of Seneca College. Extensive grounds are spread over rolling hills and covered by an attractive forest of pine and hardwood. In its midst is the turreted stone Eaton Hall, which overlooks the lake and is used by the college to host conventions.

The second estate in the area is the Marylake Shrine, home of the Augustinian Seminary. From Eaton Hall return to Eversley and turn right onto Sideroad 15. At the next crossroads, you will come to an arching stone gate. But it is a gate that never closes, for the grounds are freely open to the public—provided no one disturbs the order's sanctuaries. Drive through the gates and follow the lane as it winds through a tunnel of spruces. Where the woods give way to pasture (the group raises Herefords) you will see a massive red brick barn. Then the lane forks: the right branch leads to the stone religious retreat house, a private area; the left takes you to the modern seminary and church. Here again, the Eaton touch is felt: the organ in the shrine once rested in Eaton Hall. The site itself is the original farm and summer home of Sir Henry Pellatt, builder of Toronto's Casa Loma. Beyond the buildings is a placid pond called Mary Lake. Although the grounds are open, this is not a park. You may stroll and photograph, but you should not picnic.

Most of the side roads that lead west from the seminary have been blocked by Highway 400. The most attractive place to cross the highway is through the old village of Kettleby, which you can reach by driving 7 km north from the seminary gates. (Kettleby lies 1 km west of Keele Street on Kettleby Road.) Unlike other north-leading roads, Keele Street is lightly travelled. The road begins to rollercoaster as it enters the steep hills that typify the ridge. Although new country homes now dominate the old pastures, watch for the old farmhouses, many of them dating back to the 1840s and 1850s.

## Kettleby

Kettleby has changed little since its early days. Many of its original buildings line the treed main street, though several have found new uses. The Methodist church built in 1873 has become an antique store. However, the stone Anglican church (erected in 1891) still opens for worship each Sunday. The general store is now the Kettleby Italian bakery, while across from it are two handsome early houses, Brunswick Hall and Curtis House.

From the store the road winds down the hill and into the little valley that once hummed with gristmills and a distillery. It is now a grassy meadow.

## Kettleby to Palgrave

Continue west across Highway 400 and, at Weston Road, turn left. A busy artery, it leads you quickly to the next portion of the ridge backroad. When you have gone 7 km on Weston Road, watch for the 15th Sideroad and turn right. Because the great ridge blocked most roadbuilders, only Weston Road brings you to its southern face in this area. Continue on the 15th Sideroad to the 7th Concession Road, where you will encounter the southerly thrust of the ridge and a landscape of rugged hills that have attracted still more country estates.

Turn right onto the 7th Sideroad. It leads you northward to the ridge that deflects it westward onto the 16th Sideroad.

Just beyond the bend you will pass a once active

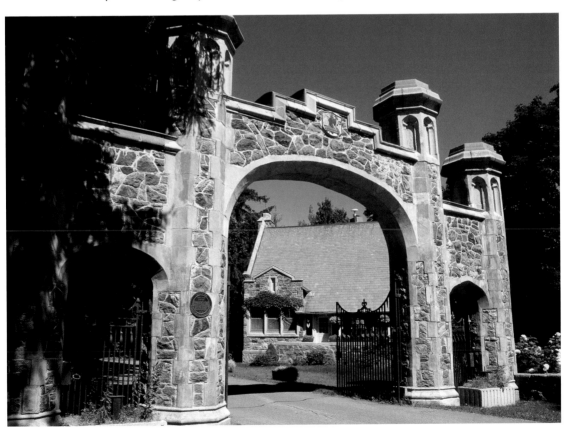

A solid gate invites entry to the Augustinian seminary grounds.

pioneer community named New Scotland. Settled in the 1830s by Archibald Kelly and a colony of Scottish immigrants, this community contained a sawmill, a blacksmith's shop, an Orange lodge and a school. Today these buildings have been replaced by spacious country estates. The only relic of the early Scottish community survives in the name of the small kettle lake at the foot of the peak, Kelly's Lake.

For the next 10 km the 16th Sideroad doglegs back and forth at intersections, through scenic sand hills and little gullies, until it ends abruptly at King Concession Road 12. Turn right here and travel 2 km to the next intersection, that with Sideroad 17. Turn left and follow it less than 1 km to Mount Wolfe Road, then turn right. For 3 km the road grinds up a steep hillside and then enters the heart of the ridge, the Albion Hills. Here the summit of Mount Wolfe overlooks a quiltwork of farms and country homes and, on the distant southern horizon, the towers of Mississauga. Although the slopes of the mountain are steep, the summit, which is home to a community of farmers, is level. On the northwest corner of the first intersection stands a well-preserved complex of traditional red barns. Turn left onto Old Church Road and drive 1.5 km across the plateau and down the side of the mountain to Mount Pleasant Road, where you turn right and remount the hill. This is the west end of Mount Wolfe, and the views from here extend both south and west. It was on its peak that the Mount Wolfe post office and church once stood. However, all that remain are the headstones preserved in a common foundation.

Continue north and descend the mountain for the last time through a hardwood forest dotted with country estates. Turn left onto Hunsden Sideroad and drive through rolling farmland to a T intersection. Turn right here onto Mount Hope Road, and then after 1 km turn left onto Pine

Avenue, which leads into Palgrave, the Albion Hills' only village.

## Palgrave

Although they are surrounded by estate subdivisions, some of Palgrave's historic buildings survive. The village was originally known as Buckstown and was first gathered around Robert Campbell's gristmill. It remained small until the Hamilton & Northwestern Railway was built through town. Then it boomed. In its heyday it contained several hotels and stores and a number of small industries. Today the industries are gone, as is the station and the rail line itself, though Campbell's millpond remains. Period houses and churches line the narrow back streets, while at the corner of Pine Street and Highway 50 Palgrave's old hotel with its three gables has remained much as it was along with two neighbouring structures. A short distance south on Highway 50 you will find the Albion Hills Conservation Area. With its fields, swimming hole and access to the Bruce Trail, it provides an opportunity to leave the car and explore the beauties of the ridge on foot.

## Palgrave to Highway 10

Today Highway 50 follows Palgrave's main street south, crossing the abandoned railway line, now converted to a scenic rail trail, to the Patterson Sideroad 25, where you turn right. Once free of the jungles of estate subdivisions, the ridge becomes a range of smaller wooded hills. Near the first crossroad, you will cross the two branches of the Humber River; 3 km farther on, at the Gore Road, sits the former village of Lockton, which now retains only its store and a log house. Continue west for 2 km to the next intersection, the Centreville Road. The road here winds around wooded hillsides and through dark gullies to the open farmland of the Centreville Road. Turn right, drive

The Caledon Rail Trail, shown here in Inglewood with the Credit Valley Flyer tour train, crosses the main street of Palgrave.

3.5 km to Finnerty Sideroad and turn left. Here the road resumes its winding way through a landscape of hills, forests, fields and new country homes. After 3 km it stops once more, this time at the busy Airport Road.

Busy even in pioneer days, when it was known as the 6th Line, this is the same Airport Road that, 40 km south, carries six lanes of traffic past Pearson International Airport. Here it carries country commuters. Turn left and drive south 2 km to the Escarpment Sideroad and turn right. The last leg of the Ridge Road, it surges over the peaks of the rugged Caledon Hills. To the south

the views extend across pastures and woodlots and culminate in the distant Metro skyline. For 9 more km you wind past fields, some overgrown, some replanted in pine, a few still grazed by slow-moving cattle. The great ridge ends abruptly at the Niagara Escarpment. So high is the ridge that at this point it has buried even that great rocky cuesta.

It is here at Highway 10 that the Ridge Road drive ends. To the left lies Brampton and, less than an hour away, Toronto. Orangeville is a short drive north, to the right.

# 8  The Ridge Road East

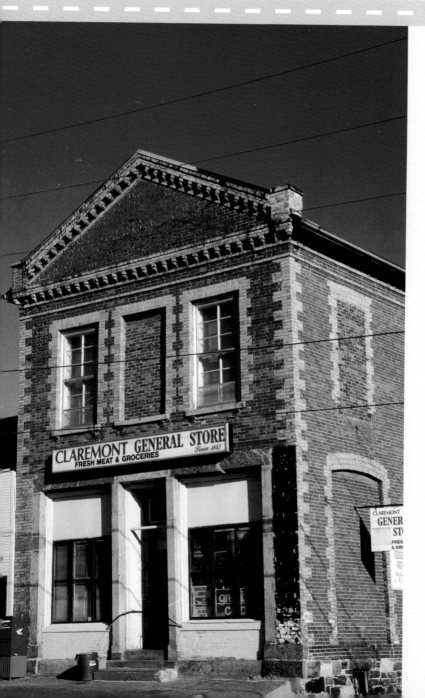

Mirroring the Ridge Road West, this scenic route wanders through the rugged Oak Ridge hill country east of Toronto. To get to your starting point, drive east from Toronto on Highway 401, exit north onto Brock Road and follow it 15 km to Claremont. The tour follows a series of gravel concession roads and side roads easterly for about 50 km to Highway 35/115 at a point 3 km north of Kirby (the hamlet where Backroads Route 9, the Rice Lake Road, begins).

In contrast to the Ridge Road West, there are fewer estate homes on this trip and more of the simple settlers' farmsteads and churches. And although the views are less spectacular, the hills are more rugged, the gulches deeper and darker. So difficult is some of the terrain that many early roads have been abandoned.

Again, this is a tour for the recreational driver who wants a country getaway.

**The eastern Ridge Road passes the historic general store in Claremont.**

The story of this area closely parallels that of the Ridge Road West. Although the lakeshore area was bustling with farms by 1810, the steep hills discouraged the movement of pioneers inland until after 1830. By then the government had constructed a few crude roads over low spots in the hills. But being a headwater area, the region had few mill sites, and many of those that did attract mills dried up shortly after the forest was cleared. As a result the landscape is one of abandoned farms, rough pastures and small villages and hamlets that have long lost their functions and have largely disappeared (though in recent years some have become dormitory communities for commuters to such cities as Oshawa, Whitby and even Toronto).

## Claremont

There are two Claremonts: Old Claremont: the original crossroads village; and Claremont Siding, which came into existence after 1884, when the Ontario & Quebec Railway, now the Canadian Pacific Railway, was built through the settlement.

As Brock Road approaches Claremont, it leaves its original route and bypasses the village. Continue past Durham Road 5 to the north end of the bypass. Turn left twice to Claremont Siding. At the crossing the station is long gone, a victim of the CPR's heritage policy, though one of its original feed mills still stands. Across the track, forlorn yet solid, a brick carriage factory hugs the roadside. Along the side streets and the road to Old Claremont are the large homes of the early railway days.

The settlement of Old Claremont lies 1 km from the crossing and contains this route's most interesting building. Here, where the Brock Road intersected an important side road, now Regional Road 5, an early settler named Noble built a general store. Known at first as Noble's Corners, the community had little more than a couple of stores and a hotel. But when the railway arrived to the north, the back streets of Old Claremont filled with houses and more businesses moved to the village. Many still stand on these narrow roads and today mix with newer homes.

As Claremont gradually became a dormitory town to Oshawa, its residents paid less attention to their own stores. Now most shops are shuttered or serving a different purpose. Three of the four corners of the Old Claremont crossroads have been stripped of their original buildings, but the fourth boasts the most ambitious country general store in central Ontario. Built in 1847 by John Mitchell, this large two-storey building with its elaborate brick facade greets today's visitors little changed, and it is still a general store.

## Claremont to Glen Major

Drive east from the store on Durham Road 5. Here several old village buildings line the street. Two blocks from the store is the 1865 brick Baptist church. Since leaving Brock Road you have made three left turns, bringing you back to Brock Road, also called Durham Road 1.

From Durham Road 1, continue east on Durham Road 5 and drive across the south face of the ridge for 5.2 km to a historic crossroads hamlet called Balsam.

Halfway to Balsam, two bridges cross the tumbling headwaters of Duffin Creek, which was once the power source for countless mills. The creek is now the focus for a string of conservation areas. Conceived originally to provide flood-control measures, these extensive conservation areas fill a growing need for public recreation areas that neither the province nor the municipalities are prepared to fill. The Claremont Conservation Area lies just 2 km south of Durham Road 5 on Westney Road, and the Greenwood Conservation Area is just 3 km beyond that. Both offer hiking

trails, picnic areas and playing fields.

To reach Balsam, stay on Durham Road 5. This village had its origins in 1869, when J. Palmer opened a crossroads general store (including a post office) to serve the needs of area settlers. Soon the intersection added a second store, a temperance hall and a blacksmith's shop. But it failed to grow beyond that. Palmer's store closed after a few decades, though it still stands on the northeast corner of the crossroads. Graham's yellow brick store, which opened in the 1890s, is on the southeast corner and is still open for business.

At Balsam, turn north onto Balsam Road and follow it to one of the more scenic portions of this trip. For about 1 km you stay on the flatlands below the hills. But after you cross the railway tracks, the scenery changes dramatically. As you enter the valley of Duffin Creek, the wooded hills steepen and close in on the road, forcing it onto the contours of the valley wall. About 3 km from Balsam, a string of simple homes cling to the steep slope and peer into the gulch. This is the picturesque valley village of Glen Major.

## Glen Major

Although Duffin Creek at this point is little more than a brook, its source a mere 1 km upstream, it became the focus for a busy 19th-century mill town. Because of the steepness of the hills, this area was not settled until 1840, long after the plains below. Among the first to settle here were the Sharrards, who dammed the waters of Duffin Creek to power a sawmill and a gristmill. The bustling settlement became known as Sharrards Mills. In the 1870s, E. Major acquired the Sharrards' properties and ran three sawmills and a gristmill. The settlement's name was changed to

Opposite: The Oak Ridges Moraine is home to many diverse species of plants and animals.

The little white church at Glen Major has been called one of Ontario's prettiest.

Glen Major, and the community added a church and school. But when the forests vanished, so did the mills. The ponds have survived and are now maintained by a private fishing club. Although they lie close to the road, you have no access to them. Beyond them is the village's feature attraction, at least for photographers. Built in 1873, the white board-and-batten Methodist church at the north end of the village, its simple pioneer architecture framed by a hillside of maples, is an image that earned it a place in *Steeple Chase*, a photo book on Ontario's most attractive churches.

## Glen Major to Burketon Station

North of Glen Major the road winds out of the narrow, steepening gully onto a plateau. Watch for the road sign that announces Chalk Lake Road and turn right. For 2 km the road runs through pastures and fields and past the new country homes that are sprouting on them. Then it plunges into the valley of Lynde Creek.

From the stop sign at Durham Road 23, continue straight on. Through the trees on the right you will see the sparkling waters of Chalk Lake. Ringed by steep hills, Chalk Lake's waters fill a pothole that was left by a stray piece of melting glacier 20,000 years ago. For several years it has remained an enclave of large summer homes and country estates, shielded from prying eyes by the thick hardwood forest that cloaks the hillside.

East of Chalk Lake the road returns to the crest of the ridge. Continue for 7 km to the intersection of Highways 7 and 12. Over this section of road, the rugged knolls gradually diminish, and at the intersection they have levelled off to become prosperous farmland. Highway 7/12 was an early settlement

Settlers carved their farms on Lake Ontario's shore as early as the 1790s, but four decades would pass before the frontier moved inland. By the 1830s, many of the interior lands had been opened and settlements had sprung up at key crossroads and at water power sites on the numerous streams. As long as there were forests, the sawmills prospered. Then, as the woods disappeared, the wheat years took over. But American tariffs ruined the grain trade, and by 1900 Ontario farmers had turned to dairy and beef farming. Today, this inland area remains one of family farms, quiet country villages and rural traditions.

## Kirby to Kendal

Kirby began its life during the 1850s, after the opening of the Kendal Road, and it soon became a busy crossroads hamlet. Unfortunately, highway widenings have left little of Kirby. On the west side of the highway is the 100-year-old brick former Methodist church, and beside it a house built in 1858. On the northeast is a school that has been converted into a museum.

From the exit at Kirby drive east along Durham Road 9, which was once known as the Kendal Road. It developed as a municipal toll road and opened around 1850. The first 6 km roll over gentle hills and past lush fields and a few new country homes. Then the road descends into the valley of the Ganaraska River and to the village of Kendal.

Although Kendal contains a number of newer homes, several early houses and shops still line its shady streets, preserving the appearance it must have had in its palmy days. Kendal was laid out not on the main road, but slightly to the south of it, for it was here that in 1848 Theron Dicky built his sawmill and later added a gristmill. Only 20 years later the village contained two sawmills, four shingle mills, two hotels, two churches and four stores.

Provincial Highway
County / Regional Road

The first road to the right is Church Street, and it contains the white frame United church, built in 1870, and the one-time Orange Lodge. Turn left and drive past attractive homes to Durham Road 18.

Turn left and drive back to Durham Road 9, which is also posted as the Ganaraska Road. At the 10 km mark from Kirby, look for the turn left to the Ganaraska Forest Centre. The farms that were carved onto the sandy ridge that parallels the route have been replaced by forests. From this centre you can follow hiking or cross-country ski trails through the area. The centre is 9 km north of Durham Road 9. This is also the point at which you enter Northumberland County from what was Durham Region, but the road remains number 9.

At 15 km from Kirby you enter the hamlet of Elizabethville, first settled in the 1830s, and a small stopover village at the intersection of the Kendal Road with the Decker Hollow Road. Today the Decker Hollow Road is closed and the village of Decker Hollow has vanished, as have many of Elizabethville's original buildings.

Drive east from Elizabethville and, after 3 km, watch for the sign to the Richardson Lookout. This lookout was named after the father of Ontario's conservation movement, Arthur H. Richardson. It was he who devised the notion that municipalities sharing river watersheds should pool their resources with the province to prevent flooding, to encourage improved farming techniques and to replant forests on infertile soils. A beneficial by-product has been the development of conservation areas, and small recreation parks have been established beside reservoirs and at flood control dams and old mill dams. In parks where an old mill still stands, the conservation areas have sometimes mushroomed into "pioneer villages," with nearby buildings of historical interest being moved to the park to create a living museum. And all thanks to Richardson.

From the Richardson Lookout, look north. There the irregular peaks of the great Oak Ridge indent the horizon. This 150 km mound of sand and gravel was laid down during the last ice age, 50,000 years ago, by the swirling meltwaters from two huge glaciers. The Ganaraska River pours off the ridge into the plain below you, where it has carved its gentle valley. Here lies a landscape of green fields, barns and houses.

Return to County Road 9 and continue east. For 3 km the road descends the hill into the valley of the Ganaraska River. Beside the bridge over the river are a millpond and the village of Garden Hill, once one of the busiest villages on the Kendal Road. It began in the 1830s, when one Mr. Kirkpatrick arrived and built a mill on the river. By 1880 Garden Hill had five sawmills, two gristmills, and the largest woollen mill on the river. Its population stood at 450.

Although the mills are now gone, there remain a few interesting vestiges of Garden Hill's glory days. The general store dates back to the start of the 20th century and, unlike most of its contemporaries, still retains its wooden porch. There is the old brick church and several early houses. Take a short spin around the single residential block. Little wider than a laneway and lined with trees and simple homes, the street appears much as it did during the town's heyday. Beside the pond, the conservation authority has developed one of its picnic and swimming parks.

## Garden Hill to Bewdley

Continue east from Garden Hill. This swampy lowland is the flood plain of the Ganaraska Valley, where several little tributaries seem to meander without purpose. If you had been travelling this road over a century ago, you would have been

**Opposite: A view of Rice Lake.**

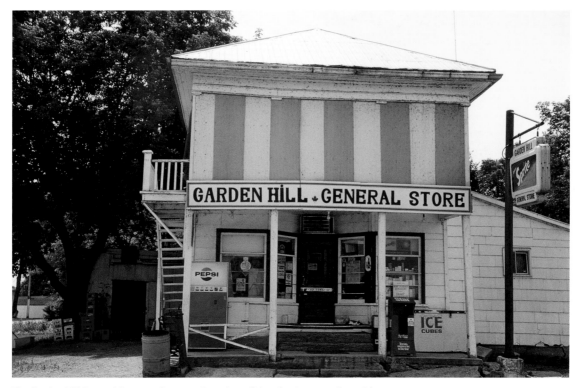

The Garden Hill General Store carries on an Ontario tradition that is generations old.

stopped 1 km east of Garden Hill and asked for a toll. The tollgate was at the intersection with one of the earliest roads to penetrate the interior from the lake, the Port Hope–Millbrook Road. Here, too, was an early mill settlement called Waterford, but, like the tollgate, Waterford has disappeared.

After 2 km, look on the right for a large white building with a porch, originally a general store and post office. Opposite this building is a white frame hall. This building was the centre of Campbellcroft, a village that began with Thomas Campbell's mill but did not take off until the late 1850s, when the first steam engine of the newly opened Midland Railway putt-putted across the road. The place was renamed Garden Hill Station and became an important shipping centre. Lumber and grain were loaded into freight cars for the 15 km journey down to Port Hope and thence for

export to the United States or England. Apart from the old store and hall, few buildings remain from these busy times, and the village has reverted to its original name.

The next 5 km continue through the lowland, past a string of farms and country homes. From the traffic lights at Highway 28, which links Port Hope and Peterborough, travel another 1 km and turn left at Rice Lake Drive. This is the old Port Hope–Peterborough stage road, and one of its stopover towns was Bewdley.

## Bewdley

Bewdley sits at the west end of Rice Lake, one of Ontario's most beautiful lakes. Pastures and woodlands that are gentle and green roll down to the shore, and islands dot the placid waters. As the name Rice Lake implies, waving fields of wild rice once surrounded the lake's low shores. They sustained both the Native population and the pioneers. But the builders of the Trent Canal dammed the lake and drowned the rice fields.

Long and narrow, Rice Lake stretches 30 km west to east but is only 5 km across. It is fed by the Otonabee River from the north and drains east into the Trent River. Being near Ontario's urban heartland, it has become a popular destination for cottagers and boaters, but not for campers and picnickers. Ontario's park planners have fallen behind, providing only a few sizable parks on this especially suitable lake.

Like the lake itself, Bewdley is a resort area, with few indications that it was once a busy port of call for the Rice Lake steamers. Today the wharves have been replaced by an attractive lakeside park, while the pioneer Halfway House has become Rhino's Roadhouse.

## Bewdley to Gores Landing

Leave Bewdley driving south, on the road on which you entered it. After just a quarter kilometre beyond the marina, look for a road forking to the left. Here you encounter an early pioneer road, this one linking Bewdley with Plainville. FolIow it for 2 km to the intersection with County Road 9. Cross through the intersection and stay on the old pioneer road, now called Oak Ridges Drive.

As in its early days, the road bends and twists around the hills and valleys. Now paved and widened, it passes handsome family farms with their farmhouses of brick or clapboard. Here the landscape changes as you enter the land of the "whalebacks." These hills, so named for their resemblance to the smooth, elongated back of a whale, were moulded when the great glaciers re-advanced over their earlier deposits of sand and gravel. Geologists call them drumlins.

About 5 km from County Road 9 you will

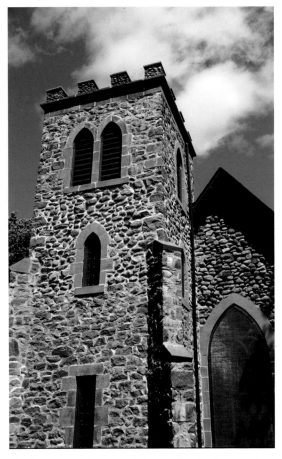

The St. George's stone church at Gores Landing is one of the most historic and picturesque along the Rice Lake Road.

encounter the Plainville United Church, which was built in 1903 as a Methodist church. Its tall steeple soars above its red brick frame in the midst of gentle farmland. About 1 km beyond it are the few houses and the feed mill of Plainville itself.

At the T intersection in Plainville, turn left onto County Road 18, cross County Road 9 and continue to the shores of Rice Lake. Here, with its century-old summer estate homes, is Gores Landing. This village began in the 1820s as a landing at the end of the Cobourg–Rice Lake Road. Stagecoaches from Cobourg and Port Hope turned passengers over to steamers such as the *Forester*, which puffed across the lake and up the Otonabee River to a fledgling mill town that would become Peterborough. Among its early travellers were Peter Robinson's Irish colonists fleeing the potato famines at home to seek the promise of Canada's wilds.

With the building in 1854 of a railway to nearby Harwood, Gores Landing lost its importance and settled down as a resort community of summer homes—a role that was reinforced during the 1950s, when the great Toronto cottage boom gobbled up the Rice Lake shoreline.

As you enter the village, follow the left fork. From this road you can see the length of the lake. Dotted across its waters are small forested islands, the crests of partly submerged whalebacks. By the water, where the high road meets the low road, are the large summer mansions of an earlier wealthy class. Built of clapboard and painted white, many are two- and three-storey houses overlooking wide green lawns. From a small park where the two roads meet, Church Hill Road leads left. Along this remnant of a former shore road is St. George's Church, a small stone building that is one of the most photographed churches in the Rice Lake area and, incredibly, once threatened with demolition.

## Gores Landing to Harwood

As you continue east from Gores Landing, you come to the historic Victoria Inn. It was constructed in 1902 by renowned Canadian artist Gerald S. Hayward, who named it The Willows. It yet retains its iconic tower and landscaping and today offers comfortable rooms and fine dining.

Continue along the shore road, County Road 18. For the next 4 km, between Gores Landing and Harwood, the road hugs the scenic shore but never allows you access. Crammed into even the narrowest beaches are cottages and campgrounds.

Harwood began as a railway town but did not remain one for long. In 1852, a group of Cobourg

merchants formed the Cobourg and Peterborough Railway. Across the shallow lake they built a 5 km trestle and causeway, much of it only a few metres above the water. On December 29, 1854, the first train rumbled across it. But after only six years the spring ice movements on the lake had so weakened the trestle that it was deemed unsafe and abandoned. Shortly afterward, it collapsed. Harwood's life as a railway town collapsed with it.

Like Gores Landing, Harwood is now a resort community, but a few vestiges have survived from

**A beautiful sunset on Rice Lake.**

the days of the railway: its main street, named Railway Street; and the remains of the causeway itself, a broken finger of fill that extends several hundred metres into the lake. You can park at a small public beach to explore the remains of the causeway. But use caution because the path is narrow and the footing tricky.

Return along Railway Street, the alignment of the old railway, to County Road 18. At this corner is the Harwood convenience store in a building that also dates from the days of rail.

There are two ways to return home. If you are bound for Ottawa or points east, stay on County Road 18 east until you reach Highway 45, where the Alderville First Nations has erected a stunning war monument. A short distance north leads you to Roseneath, with its historic carousel. Continue north on 45 to reach Highway 7 and thence Ottawa. If you are returning to the Toronto area, turn right onto Highway 45, which takes you to Highway 401, in the vicinity of Cobourg.

# 10 The Quinte Shore Road

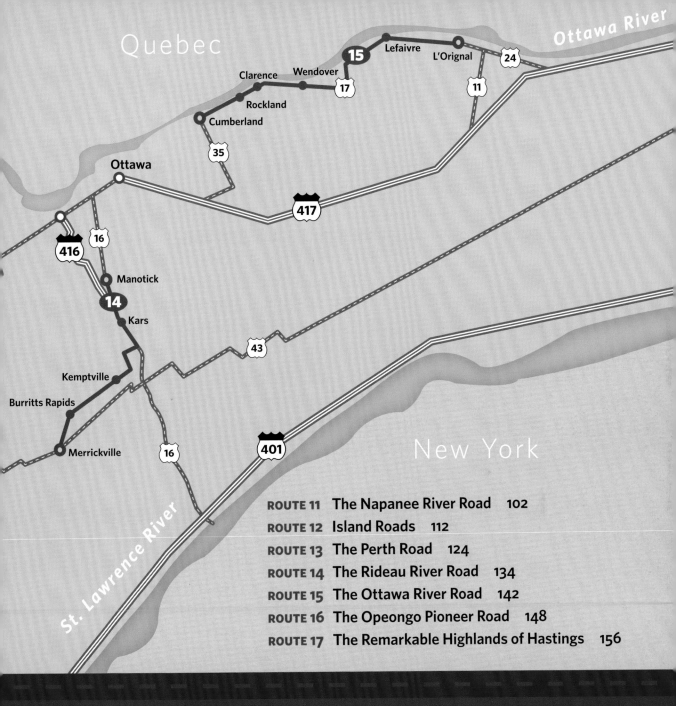

Quebec

Ottawa River

**15** Lefaivre L'Orignal **24**

Clarence Wendover **11**

Rockland **17**

Cumberland

**35**

Ottawa

**417**

**16**

**416**

Manotick

**14**

Kars

**43**

Kemptville

Burritts Rapids

Merrickville **16**

**401**

New York

St. Lawrence River

# Section 3
# Eastern Ontario

# 11 The Napanee River Road

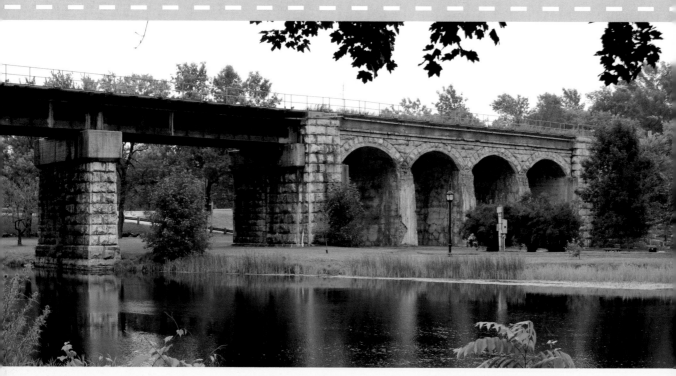

Much of Ontario's early settlement was determined by its rivers. This route probes the fertile valley of the Napanee River, which, with its string of unusual old mill villages, marks one of the thrusts of pioneering into what was then a dark and mysterious back country.

The trip begins at the Lake Ontario town of Napanee, 200 km east of Toronto, and follows the river valley 45 km north eastward. To arrive at your starting point, exit from Highway 401 at exit 579 and follow Highway 41 south into Napanee. While most of the villages you will visit contain gas stations and general stores, only Napanee has a selection of restaurants, so either snack beforehand or pack a lunch to enjoy in one of several parks.

The historic Grand Trunk railway was built over the falls that attracted Napanee's original mills.

This route contains much for you to see and do. For the photographer, stone houses, country stores and old mills provide ample subject material, while the angler can pause to cast a line in the rushing river or one of the tranquil millponds.

The gentle slopes of Lake Ontario's back shores are cut by many rivers. In a day when roads were seldom negotiable, if they existed at all, the rivers were the highways, giving early settlers their first opportunities to move inland from the communities along the lakeshore. The rivers also provided much-needed power sites for the vital sawmills and gristmills.

Yet settlement along the Napanee progressed slowly. In fact, five decades passed before the pioneers finally overcame the obstacles of rapids and windfalls and completed the settlement of the valley. While the many rapids and falls provided power sites for the early sawmills, not until the river road opened did the first settlers trudge up the fertile valley. Soon busy farms lined the concessions and the mill sites boomed into farm service towns.

Gradually the era of the mill passed and the towns declined. Today, though most of the old mills are gone, the early townscapes and farmscapes have left their imprint.

## Napanee

The outskirts of Napanee now sprawl outward to meet Highway 401. But 200 years ago there were no highways, and Napanee was little more than a sawmill settlement. At the falls on the river, Robert Clarke, Napanee's founder, built a sawmill, along with a store and a number of houses. Mill manager James Clarke gave the settlement its first name, Clarkeville, and, in 1787, he built the first gristmill between Toronto and Kingston. But Clarkeville remained small until 1812, when Allan MacPherson took over the mills and built a large store and, later, a school. By then the surrounding area was bustling with pioneer farms, and the village began to grow. In 1831 Sam Benson surveyed a townsite, and Napanee began to take the form it has today.

Drive to the stoplights at Highway 2, Dundas

Street, in the heart of Napanee, and turn left. This takes you through the business district, with commercial buildings that date back more than a century. It is a streetscape that has largely been spared from fires and much of the needless demolitions and insensitive alterations that have decimated so many Ontario towns of Napanee's size. One block north of the main street on John Street is the market square, anchored by its slender-columned town hall. Built in 1856, the hall has recently been restored and painted; it is one of the oldest in eastern Ontario.

Across the street and half a block north looms the massive red sandstone building, the Napanee post office, which was built in 1888. If you go north to John Street and then right, or east, onto Thomas Street, you will come to the Lennox and Addington County courthouse, which was built in 1864 when Napanee was proclaimed the county seat. Its cupola and pillars dominate what is otherwise a shady residential street. Behind the courthouse, and predating it by several years, is the former jail, now a museum, where you can still see the cells.

By following Dundas Street east from the downtown area and passing under the railway bridge, you will come to Clarke's old mill site, set in an appealing little riverside park. Here, at the falls in the river where Napanee began, you can enjoy a picnic before setting out on your backroads drive.

From the park retrace your steps along Dundas Street to the bridge. Watch for Camden Road and turn right. Turn right again onto Elizabeth Street and park by the historical plaque in front of a large white house. This is the mansion once owned by Napanee's co-founder, Allan MacPherson, and built around 1825. Having stayed in the MacPherson family until 1896, the house has been refurbished by the Napanee Historical Society. It provides you with a glimpse into upper-class life in early 19th-century Ontario.

## Napanee to Newburgh

Leave Napanee on Camden Road, which swings right and becomes Newburgh Road (County Road 1). After crossing Highway 401 and the Napanee River, it follows the former pioneer road up the Napanee River Valley, leading through gentle farmscapes to a string of historic mill villages.

The Greek style pillars distinguish the Napanee town hall.

The first of these is Strathcona, about 8 km from Napanee.

Strathcona owes its existence to John Thompson, who, in Windsor in 1864, perfected the modern pulp-making process. Moving to the Napanee Valley in the 1870s, he established paper mills near Camden and Newburgh, and also at Strathcona, then a tiny sawmill village known as Napanee Mills. Not only is the mill at Strathcona one of the only two in the valley to survive, but it is the only one that grew. Today, its 250 employees each day produce 130 tons of heavy paper for boxes.

Strathcona's buildings line a pair of parallel

Newburgh's main street never fully recovered from a fire that destroyed most of its buildings more than a century ago.

streets that strike westward from County Road 1 and continue up the opposite side of the river. Turn left onto County Road 16. As you cross the bridge you will see the sprawling bulk of the Strathcona mill on your right, the original section now so engulfed by additions that it is barely distinguishable. Turn right onto Finlay Street. In addition to the workers' houses, there are two outstanding stone structures—the former Methodist church, built in 1875, and the handsome two-storey public library. They face each other across the road about half a kilometre from the bridge. To resume your journey, return to County Road 1.

As you continue up the valley you will pass stone farmhouses with their wide pastures that drop gently toward the valley floor, and, after 3 km, you will come to Newburgh. At the green directional arrow turn left and drive down the valley wall into the unusual village.

## Newburgh

In contrast to Napanee and even to Strathcona, Newburgh exudes an air of quiet, a memory of days past. The streets are deserted for the most part. But it wasn't always that way.

In 1824, when David Perry built a sawmill on a waterfall in the woods, he didn't foresee a bustling mill town that would challenge Napanee for the county seat. By 1832, settlers were coming in growing numbers and soon there were factories, mills, stores and hotels in this thriving community that was known throughout the area, somewhat ingloriously, as Rogues' Hollow. Then, in the 1870s, there came John Thompson and his paper mills, and the town entered its glory days. But its

Newburgh's historic academy has survived in its pastoral setting.

booming growth was shattered when in 1887 a raging fire razed 84 buildings. By then Napanee was the county seat and the area's leading town. Most of Newburgh's destroyed industries either relocated in Napanee or were not rebuilt. More fires in 1902 and 1908 reduced the town still further, to a mere shell of its former self.

As you descend the hill to the first bridge, you will find a clutch of fine stone buildings, the only part of the main street spared by the many infernos. Here, a one-time hotel, stone stores and handsome old homes are a "must" for the photographer and historian. Cross the bridge and turn right to the conservation area that has been developed on Thompson's mill site. Here you can enjoy a lunch or stroll beside the swirling river. About half a kilometre upstream you will see the town's original railway station, a two-storey structure built by the pioneer Bay of Quinte Railway.

To see Newburgh's most celebrated building, continue north on the main street to the hardware store and turn left onto Academy St. Drive half a kilometre to the top of the hill, where you will confront a massive stone building topped by an octagonal cupola. This, the Newburgh Academy, is the oldest such institution in Ontario to survive in its original form. Started in 1839 by three local residents, it grew to become one of the province's leading teachers' colleges. The present building replaced the original in 1853, and, despite a fire in 1887, it retains its original appearance. Thanks to a fund raised by local residents and former students, the college has been restored and preserved.

This stone store is Camden East's landmark.

## Newburgh to Camden East

Retrace your trail to County Road 1. Northeast of Newburgh the valley walls retreat still farther and the pastures roll toward the river. After 3 km, you will enter the village of Camden East.

To describe Camden East as a "picture postcard" is not an exaggeration, for that is what it once was: a subject of artist Manly MacDonald for Coutts Hallmark Christmas cards.

Camden East got off to an early start, considering the difficult transportation problems that the settlers faced. By 1850 the village could claim mills, factories, stores, hotels and even a distillery. When the Bay of Quinte Railway arrived in 1871, Camden East's prosperity seemed assured. But rather than enhancing the town's trading position, the railway weakened it by putting the town in Napanee's shadow. The most striking building

in town, and one of the most remarkable on this backroad tour, is the massive grey stone hulk of a former hotel and store on the northwest corner of the main intersection, now the Bookstore Café and Antiques.

## Camden East to Yarker

As you continue east from the village, you drive by pastoral landscapes of fields and barns, as well as the river. After a little more than 6 km, County Road 1 comes to County Road 6, which bends steeply to the left and descends into the village of Yarker.

Yarker is a relative newcomer to the Napanee Valley. It began in 1840 when David Vader built a sawmill, and it received a boost nine years later when George Miller established a gristmill. The falls at one time dropped to 10 metres straight

**Two disused railway bridges at Yarker.**

down, but so consistently did the log drives wear away the soft limestone riverbed that the brink of the falls now lies 15 metres back of the base.

As Yarker grew, it attracted an array of mills and businesses and, in 1871, the Bay of Quinte Railway, which wound its way northward to Bannockburn. Four decades later, when the Canadian Northern Railway pushed the line on toward Ottawa, the village found itself on the railway's busy main line.

Although the village has slipped from its population peak of 600 to just around 400, it has retained its winding streets and many of its older buildings. The best grouping is near the corner of Water and Bridge Streets, where the former hotel stands a block from the oddly attractive Waterfall Tea Room built as M. Wright's store in 1902.

Cross the bridge and bear right on Vanluven Street, County Road 6.

## Yarker to Bellrock

As you leave the village, you pass beneath a former railway bridge that now carries the Cataraqui Rail Trail along the roadbed of the Canadian National Railway. As you proceed to Colebrook the wooded valley wall closes in from the left, while the river swirls by the road on the right.

Attracted by the landscape, country dwellers have lined the river to Colebrook with new country houses, and the two villages have become nearly one. However, you will find the heart of Colebrook beside the bridge over the river. Like Yarker and its sister river towns, Colebrook began as a sawmill village. But when the Bay of Quinte Railway passed it by, the village stagnated; what little it had was destroyed in 1877 by a fire that gutted two sawmills, three stores and five homes. Few were rebuilt, and the gaps remain.

A small park by the river has replaced the mills and provides a picnic spot. Below the dam you can still see the foundation of the gristmill, the victim of a fire in 1961. (The original mill, spared by the 1877 fire, burned in 1939.) A few metres north, the stone church, now a private residence, also escaped the conflagration. One of the village's oldest homes, and certainly its grandest, is a stone building that sits south of the bridge and faces the river.

Leave Colebrook north on County Road 6 and look for the Petworth Road sign on the right. Follow it for a little over 3 km to the least successful of the Napanee River mill towns, the ghost town of Petworth. Petworth started with a sawmill and then grew with the settlement of the area's farmlands. A stone gristmill was added in 1845, and at its peak Petworth possessed two hotels, several stores, an Orange hall, a cheese factory, a blacksmith and a carding mill. Following Petworth's demise, most of its buildings stood empty until, one by one, they succumbed to fire or were replaced by country homes. You may still see a portion of the stone foundation of the old mill. From the intersection just west of the river, drive north on German Road 3 km to a T intersection at Huffman Road and turn right. The route is narrow, passing barns and farm homes that date back more than a century.

Suddenly the road plunges into the Portland Swamp. Dense woods rise overhead as the Napanee River divides into a myriad of small tributaries that wind aimlessly through the bush. Although the swamp is over 10 km long, your crossing is less than 2 km. The road then rises from the swamp to meet County Road 7 and the unusual little village of Bellrock.

## Bellrock

Bellrock rose on the fortunes of the Rathbun Lumber Company. One of the logging giants of the 1800s, Rathbun logged the area and drove or shipped the logs to its mills at Deseronto on the Bay of Quinte. Bellrock grew not only into a supply centre for the Rathbuns but also into a milling centre in its own right. In addition to hotels, stores, a blacksmith's and a cheese factory, the village also had two sawmills, one gristmill and a carding mill, all powered by the rushing falls on the Napanee River. And one still survives. By the river stands a sawmill built in the 1920s. Under the same roof were a shingle mill and a gristmill. Once operated by the local conservation authority, the building is now vacant.

This finale to the trip is appropriate, for mills such as these created the towns on the Napanee River and brought prosperity to the valley.

To return to Kingston or points east, travel east on County Road 7 to Highway 38, which leads south to Kingston and Highway 401. If you are returning to the Ottawa area, take Highway 38 north to Highway 7 and east to the nation's capital. For returning Torontonians, travel west on County Road 7, which becomes County Road 14 on entering Lennox and Addington County. After 20 km you will come to Highway 41, which you take south to Highway 401.

**Opposite: Water power once drove the saws at the Bellrock sawmill.**

# 12 Island Roads

If you really want a break from life in the fast lane, try following some backroads that you cannot drive to. You need to take a ferry to get to the backroads of Lake Ontario's largest island communities—Wolfe, Amherst and Howe Islands. A side trip to the smaller Simcoe Island also awaits you on this route.

These low limestone outcroppings crowding the outlet of Lake Ontario and the beginning of the St. Lawrence River are linked to the mainland near Kingston by frequent ferries. While Wolfe Island provides a full range of services for any traveller, Howe and Amherst have only small stores and few gas pumps.

Allow half a day to visit each island. You can base yourself in Kingston, which has the best collection of early 19th-century stone buildings west of Montreal.

This is a trip for the traveller who likes tranquility. On these islands you may stop in the middle of the road to take in a view without fear of an impatient horn behind you. Just as there is little traffic, there has been less pressure to demolish old farmhouses and stores. So if you love the simple architecture of the 19th century, you can find it here, often little changed. On these island backroads you can take in both history and scenery, all at your own pace.

**Opposite: A few of the many Thousand Islands in the St. Lawrence River.**

Island backroads are traffic-free.

Wolfe, Howe and Amherst Islands were originally within the Seigneury of Cataraqui, which was once held by the Sieur de La Salle. After the British conquest of Canada in 1760, the islands passed to the British, though settlement did not begin until half a century later.

As the 19th century progressed, all three islands developed rapidly. The once-brooding forests were stripped clean and replaced by busy farms. Any cove that could shelter a schooner soon sprouted a wharf to ship wheat, barley or timber. Wolfe Island's population peaked at 3,600 in 1860, while the populations of Amherst and Howe peaked at 850 and 400, respectively. Each island was incorporated as a separate municipality.

With the turn of the century, urbanization reduced farm populations everywhere, and the populations of Lake Ontario's island communities plummeted to less than half their peak totals. Today, the pace of island life remains leisurely. Traffic is light and the islanders have time to chat, even with a backroader from the mainland.

## Howe Island

Howe Island is a flat limestone plateau about 9 km long and 4 km wide. Its roads follow the shore, offering views of the historic farmsteads and the sparkling waters of the St. Lawrence River.

To get to the island, leave Kingston on Highway 2 and travel east 15 km to Howe Island Ferry Road. Turn right and follow the signs to the dock. Here the 15-car cable ferry *County of Frontenac* shuttles back and forth nonstop during busy periods and on request when traffic is light. It takes only ten minutes to complete the crossing.

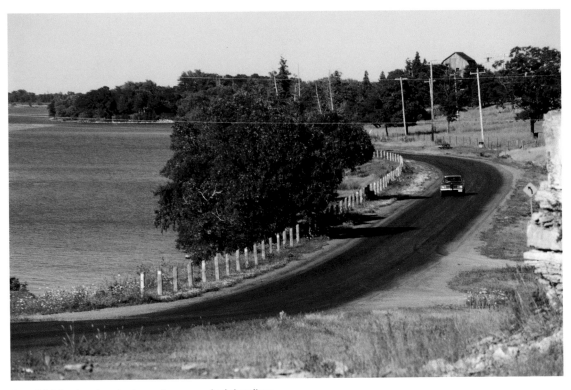

Ontario's island roads enjoy tranquil wave-washed shorelines.

Howe Island has only four main roads, two that hug the north and south shores, and two that connect them. At the dock on Howe Island, you will find a small general store and picnic benches. From the dock travel south and turn left at Shore Road, the first crossroad. This road was built to link the waterfront farms, and it winds through rolling pastures and past once busy farmsteads. After a little more than 1 km, look on the right for St. Patrick's School, which was built in 1894 and is now owned by the volunteer fire department. It is the only survivor of the island's three public schools. Although it has lost its bell tower, it appears today as its pupils might remember it.

Shortly after passing the school, you will come to a fork in the road. Keep left and pass more handsome century-old farms. As you skirt and then descend the steep limestone cliff that forms the north shore of the island, you will be treated to pleasant views of the mainland. Here the island's northern coast is interrupted by an inlet called variously Johnson Bay and Big Bay, and the farm road ends. Return all the way to the ferry road and turn left onto County Road 22.

After 2 km, you will come to the south shore. Here, at a T intersection, turn left. As the road winds in and out of the little coves, you can look across the St. Lawrence River to the Wolfe Island shore. Beside the water is a line of new cottages and country homes, occupied by Kingston commuters and seasonal occupants.

After 1 km look for a pair of renovated log cabins, one on the left beside the road and the other on the right close to the water. These are original settlers' cabins, and they are the oldest homes on the island. Over the next 2 km you will pass,

almost imperceptibly, more than a dozen former farm lots. Although they are not very wide, they are nearly 1 km deep and represent an old waterfront survey technique that, in the days before roads, insured that every settler had access to water. Of the 40 or so original farms, there are now fewer than a half-dozen.

Halfway along the south shore drive, you will encounter the island's most imposing building, St. Philomena's Roman Catholic Church. Built in 1858, it is the only island structure that was built with local limestone. Continue driving east, and, after 2 km, you will come to the island's oldest store. No longer in business, it was operated by the Goodfriend family for more than a century. The final 2 km bring you to the end of the Howe Island drive and the three-car township ferry back to the mainland.

## Wolfe Island

Shaped like a long-handled dipper, Wolfe Island is the largest of the islands and the closest to Kingston, the richest agriculturally, and the most populous. It is connected by ferry not only to Kingston, but also to Cape Vincent in New York State. Although Wolfe Island is busier than Amherst or Howe, it contains quiet coves and unhurried farm lanes. Among its more interesting features are its photogenic stone halls, houses and hotels, many of which predate Confederation itself. Two side trips—to Simcoe Island and to Garden Island—can be taken from Wolfe.

The 55-car *Wolfe Islander III* leaves Kingston from the dock at the corner of Ontario and Barrack Streets. It makes 20 crossings a day during the navigation season, but you should expect to wait your turn on a holiday weekend. Even on a

regular summer weekend, it is wise to arrive early. The crossing takes 20 minutes, and time passes too quickly.

As the ferry glides toward Wolfe Island's wooded shore, the buildings of Marysville, the island's only village, appear through the trees. On arrival, follow the ramp to the stop sign at Marysville's main street. Here most of the ferry traffic turns right to follow County Road 95 to island homes or the Cape Vincent ferry. The forest of wind turbines that rises above the flat landscape evokes an "other-worldly" feel to the pastoral island.

From the dock you should turn left onto County Road 96 and head toward the less populated "panhandle," the island's long peninsula that juts into the St. Lawrence River.

After a little more than 1 km, the road crosses what appears to be a weedy ditch. Incredibly, this was once a ship canal. In 1857, in an attempt to attract barge and schooner traffic, the Wolfe Island Railway and Canal Company sliced a 2 km canal through the island's narrowest point, eliminating the longer passage around the tip of the peninsula. But steamers had already begun to replace barges and schooners, and in 1870 the company abandoned the narrow canal. It never did build a railway.

Continue east on County Road 96, the main road, as it zigzags through the maze of old farm concession roads that crisscross the panhandle. After 3 km, follow the sharp bend to the right and then, after another 2 km, another sharp bend to the left. At the next crossroads you enter what was known as the Scotch Block Settlement, where a band of hopeful Scottish immigrants moved during the 19th century. The road passes an area of shallow soils, where farms and homesteads were abandoned. Another 4 km of twists and turns lead to the Scotch Block's Christ Church. Built in 1862 with

Despite its small size, Howe Island's church is a grand building.

**An early schoolhouse on Howe Island.**

local limestone, the church has seen steady worship ever since. From the church, continue east for 7 km to Port Metcalfe. Here the panhandle narrows to a width of only one or two farm lots. You can still see many of the original shoreline farms that were built when the water was the only highway. Port Metcalfe is the end of the road. You will need to retrace your route to return to Marysville.

## Marysville

At some point during your visit to Wolfe Island, walk around Marysville. The town started as a landing in 1802, though very few settlers arrived before the 1820s. The original wharf stood three blocks to the east of the present ferry dock, approximately where the Wolfe Island marina now sits. On the south side of the street, across from the old wharf, is the renovated General Wolfe

Hotel. Built in 1860, it has served Marysville for a century and a half. Today, it offers nine guest-rooms and a 130-seat dining room.

Walk west along Main Street and at the southeast corner of Main and Division Streets you will see a small limestone building. This is Wolfe Island's original town hall, built in 1850, just nine years after the island was incorporated as a separate municipality. It is one of Ontario's oldest and most attractive township halls. At the next corner is a red brick store, built in 1878 by Edward Baker and in the same family for more than a century. One block farther on is the village's oldest building—and one of the oldest buildings on the island. In 1832 Archibald Hitchcock built a wharf and a stone hotel, which he called the Hitchcock House. Two-and-a-half storeys high, it was constructed of local stone; the frame addition on the back came later.

The interesting old town hall on Wolfe Island.

## Simcoe Island

If you want to leave the traffic behind altogether and enjoy a short drive to view an historic lighthouse, then tiny Simcoe Island is ideal, for it has only 3 km of road. From the ferry dock in Marysville, follow County Road 96 west for 4 km until you reach the ferry landing. The two-car ferry has a schedule that coincides with the *Wolfe Islander* (for car drivers, so cyclists might miss the departure). On the island, follow the only road west. Although it's a narrow gravel road, it is in good condition. The lighthouse is at the end of the road. Constructed of local limestone about a century ago, it no longer guides vessels through the shoal-strewn waters. Because it rests on private land, there is no access to it, but it is easily viewed from the road.

## Garden Island

Garden Island is unique. For three-quarters of a century, this tiny island housed a busy shipbuilding community and was home to nearly 700 people.

The shipyards were begun in 1835 by an American named Dileno Dexter Calvin, and they continued to be run by that family until 1926. During this period the family launched 25 ships, ranging from barges to ocean vessels. The wharf and shipyards were clustered at the eastern end of the island, while the workers' simple frame homes lined a road that ran down the middle. By 1866 the population had grown large enough to have its own school, church and post office—and even its own municipal council. But when the shipyards closed, the population dwindled. Some people remained, and they proudly preserved many original structures.

There is no public access to this private domain.

Still standing are the office (with its cupola), the former post office, and the mansions of the owners: the White House of Ira Brock; and the Green House, home of the Calvins themselves. And still on the now grassy main street are some of the simpler workers' houses.

Garden Island is a museum piece, the only example of a 19th-century shipbuilding centre to survive in such remarkable condition. However, because no public authority assumes responsibility for it, its accessibility to heritage enthusiasts depends utterly on the invitation of its occupants.

## Amherst Island

The ferry for Amherst Island leaves from Millhaven, 18 km west of Kingston on Highway 33. You will be unlikely to find a lineup here, for Amherst Island, about half the size of Wolfe Island, is the most tranquil of the three main islands and has the fewest cottages and commuters.

The new *Frontenac II* glides away from the dock every hour on the half-hour and has a capacity for 33 cars. Half an hour later, the engines rumble into reverse and the gangway clangs onto the dock of the island's main village of Stella.

The roads of Amherst Island wind along windswept coastlines and cross lush farmlands. Happily, the lack of development pressure has left a legacy of farmsteads and churches. So light is the traffic that even driving for its own sake becomes a pleasure. Whether you explore the village of Stella before or after your drive, be sure to set aside a little time for that purpose.

From the ferry dock, drive a few metres to the intersection and turn left. On the corner is the small general store and post office, which has occupied the site for more than a hundred years. So have some of the buildings near it: the public library in the former Methodist church, and the Orange hall.

Continue east as the road leaves the village to follow the shore. On your left you will see the former Miller General Store, the site of Amherst Island's original landing. Look on McDonald's Lane for the historic "Lodge on Amherst Island."

Amherst Island's only link with mainland Ontario is its ferry.

The net racks are dry now as the former fishing colony on Amherst Island has largely moved on.

After 1.5 km you will come to Preston Cove. Here, tucked beside the shore, are two early estates, among the oldest homes on the island.

The road now mounts a low mesa, offering views over the North Channel to the treed mainland. A large stone house on the left, the Poplar Dell B&B, is one of the island's oldest estates. (As of this writing it may not be open.) After 2 km the road bends right, leading you 1.5 km to the south shore where the road edges so close to the low limestone shore that, during a southerly blow, waves spray across the roadway. On the landward side you will pass a string of old family farms, most of them originating a century ago or more.

When you reach Stella Road on your right, continue straight ahead on Long Point Road, which leads to Emeric Point—the site of the island's last fishing operation. Most of the old fishermen's cabins are now seasonal dwellings. From this point you can return to Stella Road and turn left toward Stella.

After 1.5 km, you will come to a handsome gothic church set against a backdrop of maples.

This is St. Paul's Anglican Church, built in 1884, its grey limestone blocks having been wrenched from a quarry at Kingston Penitentiary by sweating convicts. Continue past the church for less than 1 km and then turn left to follow the 2nd Concession, one of only two interior farm roads on the island. Here the fields have been stripped of their forest cover and the farmers carry on in much the same way as those in earlier generations.

When you reach Emerald Road, 3 km later, turn right. A farther 1.5 km will bring you into the tiny one-time port of Emerald. Once a busy shipping village, it died with the grain trade. From Emerald you can see across the north channel to the low shoreline of Bath, now dominated by the chimneys of a generating station.

Once you have returned to the mainland and joined the rush of traffic home, you will soon realize why the Howe Islanders, the Wolfe Islanders and the Amherst Islanders are in no hurry to trade the "inconveniences" of island life for life in the fast lane.

Overleaf: Sailing is popular off the shores of Wolfe Island.

# 13 The Perth Road

Two of Ontario's best-preserved stone towns, Kingston and Perth, are linked by one of its most historic backroads. This 80 km paved road grinds over granite ridges and swoops into villages nestled in valleys. Along the way are barns, churches, general stores, a railway station and a ghost town. There are water holes to fish in and parks to picnic in. So pack well for this trip, taking fishing rod, camera and a picnic lunch.

Perth's turning basin was severed from the main Rideau Canal when short-sighted county politicians built a bridge too low for vessels to pass under.

The Perth Road began as a settlement road. Although both Kingston and Perth were growing towns by 1820, and in full bloom by 1850, the land between them lay empty and neglected. The opening of the Rideau Canal in 1832 brought settlers to the shores of the Rideau lakes, and there Westport grew. The government then hired the Kingston and Perth Road Company to survey and cut a road northward from Kingston to Perth, finally opening the interior. By 1854, however, the road had progressed only 20 km, and in 1860 a series of lawsuits forced the company to relinquish its contract. The government came to the rescue and completed the road.

## Kingston to Perth Road Village

Before leaving Kingston, allow time to visit its numerous historic sites and to sample its small but growing contingent of fine restaurants. Leave Kingston north on Division Street. Or, if you are exiting directly from Highway 401, do so at Exit 617 (Division Street) and turn left at the stoplights at the bottom of the ramp and onto the Perth Road.

The first portion of the route passes through a flat limestone plain, where early stone farmhouses mingle with the rural sprawl that emanates from Kingston. Soon after starting your trip you will see on your left, about 2 km north of Highway 401, the entrance to the Little Cataraqui Creek Conservation Area. This park is a nature reserve with nearly 20 km of hiking trails.

Continue north for 8 km. Here you will pass the large old farmhouses and the fertile countryside that gave birth to a prosperous farming community and the village of Inverary.

About 5 km north of Inverary, a striking transition occurs. As the road descends a steep hill it suddenly leaves behind the flat limestone plain and enters the rugged granite landscape that typifies the Canadian Shield. Rocky knobs jut from the earth as forest replaces the pastures and cornfields. The line of demarcation is the linear Loughborough (pronounced locally "Lober") Lake. This lake is so narrow where you cross it that you may easily mistake it for a river. Beside the bridge a public boat ramp provides you with a place to cast for a few bass or perch. From the bridge continue north, where you will pass the last pocket of good farmland on the southern portion of the road. Another 5 km bring you to the village of Perth Road.

If this had not been the site of the Perth Road's first tollgate, there would probably not have been a village here at all. County Road 10 now bypasses the quiet little place, and to reach it you will need to turn off at the directional arrow. With its old houses, churches and former store, Perth Road village has altered little over the years. At the village intersection is the former Perth Road general store, a red brick building that 100 years ago was the Jabez Stoness Hotel.

## Perth Road Village to Bedford Mills

As you leave the village you cross the now-abandoned right-of-way of the Canadian Northern Railway. Built in 1912 to connect Toronto with Ottawa, the line was abandoned and the track lifted by its most recent owner, CN Rail.

Continue along County Road 10. As you drive the next 25 km section of the route, with its bare rocks and weedy ponds, you will understand why many settlers shunned the area. The few who tried have left a legacy of overgrown clearings and sagging barns, many of which you can see to this day. However, the maze of lakes has attracted summer cottagers and restored some prosperity; yet, aside from a pair of boat ramps, there is no public access to the lakes.

## Bedford Mills

After more than 15 km from Perth Road village, watch for an orange-and-blue historical marker pointing to Bedford Mills, and follow it left. This narrow dirt track was the original Perth Road alignment up to Bedford Mills. From a high granite ridge, Buttermilk Falls cascades into a back bay of Loon Lake. Here, in the 1830s, Benjamin Tett built a sawmill. Not only was there water power to drive the mill, but Loon Lake led directly into the Rideau Canal. When the long-awaited Perth Road finally arrived and settlers moved in, Tett added a store and a gristmill to serve the new community. Bedford Mills boomed and, at its peak, could claim a powerhouse, a church, numerous private dwellings, and a cheese factory. But after the turn of the century most of the buildings shut down and many of the residents moved away. The place is now a ghost town.

You will probably want to spend some time photographing the site. The mill is a private residence, but its location beside both the road and the pond makes it an ideal photo subject. Avoid trespassing. Near the mill stands the one-time powerhouse, its flume still visible in the falls. St. Stephen's Church still stands, though services are held only in the summer. Beside the church is the plaque that summarizes the history of the quiet little mill village.

## Bedford Mills to Westport

Continue along the gravel road for a short distance until it returns to County Road 10, then turn left. The road soon leaves the rocky highlands and once more enters an area of fertile farmlands, those that surround the Rideau Lakes. In this geological basin a pocket of silty and fertile soils has

**Opposite:** The gristmill at Bedford Mills is one of this ghost town's few surviving structures.

Perth's main street.

corner is St. James Anglican Church, built in a high-steepled gothic style in 1881. Beside it sits the courthouse, erected in 1842. On the courthouse lawn are two 200-year-old cannons that have seen action in three wars. On the northeast corner is another of Perth's most celebrated houses, Summit House, built in 1823 for James Boulton, Perth's first lawyer. It was modelled after Toronto's famous Grange, now a part of the Art Gallery of Ontario.

A right turn takes you back to Gore Street and what is perhaps Perth's most famous house, the McMartin House dating from 1839.

From Harvey Street, walk south one block to Craig Street. One block west on Craig sits the legendary Inge-Va. Set back from the road beneath a canopy of willows and maples, with its stone walls and delicate fretwork, it has been described as Ontario's most beautiful house.

It was also the site of Ontario's last fatal duel. In 1833, two young law students, John Wilson and Robert Lyon, confronted each other with duelling pistols. When the smoke cleared from the early morning air, Lyon lay mortally wounded.

Perth contains much more to see. But if you are ready to rest your feet, you can do so in the neatly landscaped Stewart Park behind the town hall. And if you want a meal Perth has a variety of restaurants, many in the old stone buildings that make Perth one of Ontario's most historic towns.

At the corner of Herriott and Wilson Streets, a restaurant occupies the Code's Mill across from Stewart Park and a statue of Canada's legendary race horse Big Ben, and his rider Ian Miller.

Opposite: A riverside setting in downtown Perth.

# 14 The Rideau River Road

This short route, just 45 km long, follows the Rideau Canal between two early mill towns, Manotick and Merrickville. Most of the villages on this route are exceptionally rich in historic buildings, so be prepared to do some walking.

**Actors in period costumes perform a gun salute during the opening day of the Watson's Mill Museum in Manotick.**

shop. Built in 1870, this mansard-roofed frame shop was originally a village store and a popular gathering spot for the townsfolk.

If you wish to know more about Dickinson Square's many historic buildings, visit the Manotick website at www.manotick.ca.

## Manotick to Kars

Follow Mill Street to Main Street, which becomes Rideau Valley Drive, and turn left. Here are Manotick's more modern amenities, including restaurants and gas stations. As you leave the village you will see how the banks of the Rideau have attracted Ottawa commuters, who have converted the shore into an expensive Ottawa suburb. Five km from Manotick, Rideau Valley Drive bends right to follow Roger Stevens Drive to an intersection. Turn left and continue on Rideau Valley Drive to enter the 150-year-old hamlet of Kars.

## Kars

With its parklike river bank, its narrow streets, and its 19th-century homes and shops, Kars beckons you to amble, to photograph and, perhaps, to picnic or cast a line from the wharf. Drive through the village and turn left onto Wellington Street, a road that leads to the water.

Kars traces its origins back to 1829, the year James Lindsay arrived and, a little to the south of the present dock, built a wharf to ship lumber. Three years later the Rideau Canal brought a commercial boom, and Lindsay's wharf became a busy spot. North of the wharf, a six-street town plot was laid out and named Wellington. It became the focus for the homes, shops and churches that collected at the site. But in 1854, when the railway shunned Kars, the community's growth faltered, and to this day the village has changed little.

From the wharf, walk back along Wellington

Street two blocks to Nelson Street. These waterside blocks retain their narrow streets and their canopy of trees. At the northeast corner of Wellington and Nelson Streets is Adam Eastman's old home. Built in 1854 by one of the settlement's first mill owners, this white frame house still has its original windows with their irregular panes. Walk north on Nelson two blocks to Anne and turn left to Rideau River Drive, the main street. Just north of the corner is St. John's Anglican Church, a white clapboard building that was constructed by John Eastman in 1850. It is Kars's oldest church. Continue your walk south on Rideau back to the corner of Wellington Street. The house on the southeast corner is the former Zena Ault Hotel, a boisterous spot during the boom days. Return along Wellington to your car.

## Kars to Burritts Rapids

Continue south on Rideau Valley Drive. Half a kilometre from Kars, look for a stone farmhouse. This is James Lindsay's original home, built in 1829. South of Kars, the shoreline is flat. Even so, it has attracted cottagers and commuters, whose homes mingle with old farmhouses and barns. At 7 km from Kars you will come to Baxter Conservation Area, where you can picnic or even swim (if the algae growth is low enough).

From the park, Rideau Valley Drive continues west as Dulworth Road across Highway 416. Turn left onto 4th Line and then onto Regional Road 44 (or Marilyn Wilson), where you fork left over the river to the south bank. Here your route leads to the right onto River Road. If forestry or hiking interests you, drive instead straight south from River Road to the Ferguson Forest Centre. This 300 hectare tree garden offers hiking and gives tours during the year.

Then, back at the bridge, drive west on River Road 12 to County Road 23. Turn right and drive

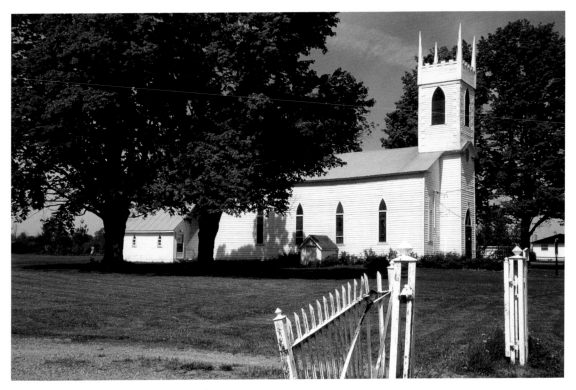

Burritts Rapids' attractive frame Christ Church.

across the bridge for one of the highlights of the trip, the village of Burritts Rapids.

## Burritts Rapids

Beside the road you will find Burritts Rapids lock 17. As part of Parks Canada's preservation efforts, the locks are operated by hand, as they have been since 1832. But the village predates even the canal.

In 1793 two Loyalist brothers, Stephen and Daniel Burritt, fled from Arlington, Vermont, and made their way up the Rideau River to a set of rapids, which they felt could power their mills. By the time the Rideau Canal opened, nearly 40 years later, Burritts Rapids was a flourishing mill village. But the railways bypassed the village, businesses fled and, for years, many buildings stood empty. Today, most are residences maintained by owners who care for the past.

From the lock continue to Grenville Street and turn right to cross the swing bridge and continue north up Grenville Street. Here the tight rows of wooden 19th-century homes and former businesses present a century-old streetscape. At Centre Street you will find the old hotel and old village homes. Venture down the side streets and you will find a row of simple frame cabins, a large white frame house with an elaborately fretted wrap-around porch that architects call gothic revival, and a 150-year-old Methodist church that is now a private home. Then continue north to the next bridge. In a small park beside the river is a plaque commemorating the founding of the village. Beside it is a former store that now contains a community centre.

At the head of Grenville Street, set back from the road in a large churchyard, is Christ Church,

The Jakes Block is a downtown Merrickville landmark.

one of eastern Ontario's most photographed churches. It was built in 1831. A square crenellated tower soars above its white frame body, and in its gable is an unusual circular window. The cemetery surrounding the church contains headstones that date back more than a century and a half.

## Burritts Rapids to Merrickville

From Burritts Rapids return to the south side of the river and continue west on River Road, County Road 23. This quiet road winds along the Rideau's swampy shores past century-old riverside farms and several handsome houses, some of brick but many of them built by the Scottish stonemasons who laboured for John By to build the Rideau Canal. But one in particular is strikingly different. At 2 km from Burritts Rapids the road bends left and then back to the right. At this

second bend, watch for the house set back on the left. While its storey-and-a-half style is typical, its alternating pattern of red and yellow bricks is found among only a few old houses and is unique to this area.

Here the river's banks are steeper, its flow swifter. Over the next 6 km the river plunges so steeply that the canal builders had to construct four separate sets of blocks. Just past the house is the entrance to the Poonamalie Locks, and half a kilometre beyond that are the Nicholson Locks, with a bridge and side road to Andrewsville.

Founded in the 1830s by Rufus Andrews, Andrewsville grew into a busy mill village with a store, a cheese factory and a population of 150. The mill is gone and fewer than a half-dozen original houses remain, with a few new cottages and homes between them.

Return across the bridge to your route and continue to Provincial Highway 43, which takes you into Merrickville, the finale of your trip.

## Merrickville

On this particular trip the best comes last, for Merrickville's buildings, many of stone, have changed little in more than a century. Like Burritts Rapids, the town began with a Loyalist fleeing the oppression in post-Revolutionary America. William Merrick arrived in 1793 and built a sawmill at the rapids. The steep drop in the river required John By to build three sets of locks and one of his protective blockhouses. When the canal opened, Merrickvllle boomed. In 1848, Merrick's son Stephen built extensive woollen mills and a gristmill. When the railway entered town, Merrickville boomed again. Most of its present buildings date from one of these two boom periods.

The flashing light marks the corner of Main and St. Lawrence Streets and is the centre of town. Either turn left and park by the stores on St. Lawrence or continue straight ahead, past the blockhouse, and park by the river.

Merrickville is another town that is best enjoyed on foot. Start with the blockhouse. Built in 1832, it is the largest of John By's blockhouses. Like the others, it never saw military duty, and today it is a museum of military and pioneer paraphernalia.

Walk north from the blockhouse across the bridge to an island in the river, the site of Merrick's woollen mills. On one side of the island are By's locks, on the other the tumbling rapids that powered Merrick's mills. The mills operated uninterrupted from 1848 to 1954 and were slated for preservation, but a raging fire destroyed them, and Parks Canada was left with only a few limestone walls to stabilize. Cross the second bridge and walk

up the road to the driveway to William Merrick's grand mansion. Set behind stately maples, it was built with local limestone and has stood as the town's finest home since 1821.

Return across the two bridges to the town's commercial core. At the southeast corner of St. Lawrence and Main is another of Merrickville's outstanding buildings, the Jakes Block, which was built by Eleazer Whitmarsh sometime in the late 1860s. Its stone walls rise three storeys, its

**A boat in the Merrickville Locks.**

corner a graceful curve. What makes it particularly appealing is the fact that its facade has never been altered and still displays the arching doors and windows of Whitmarsh's early design. It is now the Baldachin Inn and Restaurant. The Block is architecturally balanced by another three-storey stone structure opposite it.

Inevitably, Merrickville has been discovered. How could it not? After nearing death in recent years, the business district has been revived with boutiques and cafés, especially in and near the Jakes Block.

There are many reasons to linger in the region. West of Merrickville, on Highway 43, is Smiths Falls with its extensive railway museum, and the two-storey outhouse at the Bates House Museum.

But if home beckons, then Highway 7 lies just a few kilometres to the north, and Highway 401 to the south.

# 15 The Ottawa River Road

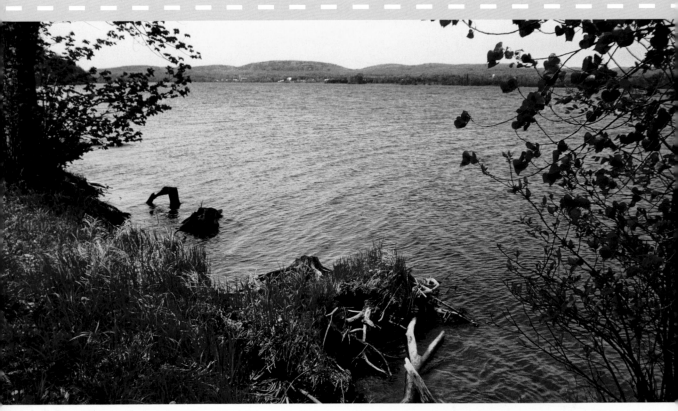

Although ski-slope roofs and silvery steeples are common in rural Quebec, they are not seen as often in Ontario. Yet many lurk along the Ottawa River Road, proudly proclaiming their French-Canadian origins. Mansard roofs crown village homes, and church steeples punch the sky. It is Ontario's French-Canadian heartland: the Ottawa River Road.

It is also a riverside drive. The road begins at Cumberland, east of Ottawa, and winds easterly along the Ottawa River shore, following paved county roads for most of its 70 km length. It ends at L'Orignal, near the Quebec border. The trip

**Views across the Ottawa River follow most of this route.**

offers breathtaking views to the mountains deep in Quebec on the opposite shore, which you can reach on any of several small ferries that shuttle across the river.

**L'Orignal's courthouse is Ontario's oldest.**

Ontario's countryside harbours many cultural groups. Few, however, have left their distinctive imprint so indelibly on the landscape as have the Franco-Ontarians of the lower Ottawa River. It is just too bad that countryside sprawl is eating away that precious heritage.

# 16 The Opeongo Pioneer Road

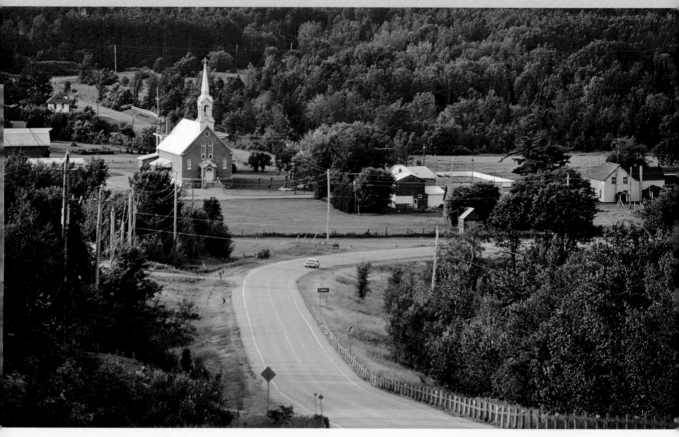

**From the heights of the Opeongo Road, the views extend across the Ottawa Valley to Quebec.**

Deep in the Black Donald Mountains of Renfrew County lies a pioneer landscape of log cabins and barns, of snaking rail fences and simple churches. Through it winds the Opeongo Road. This route begins at the town of Renfrew, 320 km northeast of Toronto and 130 km west of Ottawa, and it follows the old pioneer trail for 110 km to Barry's Bay. Fill your lunch bag and your gas tank in Renfrew, as you will find few facilities along this route.

I n 1854 Peter Vankoughnet, chief commissioner for Crown Lands, announced that the unsettled wilds of central Ontario would be thrown open for settlement. Two dozen settlement roads would breach the timbered highlands, and the land along them would be free.

The Opeongo Road, which was surveyed in 1855, was among the first of these colonization roads. Despite its deplorable condition, in its first nine years the road attracted 300 settlers. Villages sprang up at water-power sites, at stopping places and major road junctions. But the rush soon subsided. The harsh climate, the infertile soils and rumours of starvation sent prospective settlers searching for friendlier regions.

Reflecting on the road scheme's collapse, a Renfrew journalist wrote in 1900: "Immigrants who came in considerable numbers were disappointed … Those who had means mostly fled the country … those who were poorer had to stay and make the best of it." Those who did stay could scarcely afford major improvements, and so the agricultural landscape today retains the log cabins and barns of the pioneers who settled it in its early days.

## Renfrew

Although the Opeongo Road as surveyed began at Farrell's Landing on the Ottawa River, this tour starts at the McDougall Mill Museum in the town of Renfrew. The mill was built of stone fired locally by John McDougall in 1857. Inside, the museum houses a collection of 19th-century clothing, furniture, early farm tools and local artifacts. It is open daily during the summer and has picnic tables located beside the scenic gorge of the Bonnechere River.

From the mill, follow Stewart and Bridge Streets south to Raglan Street and through the main business district. Many of these solid commercial blocks were built in the late 19th century by wealthy lumbermen. One was Robert Carswell, whose baronial estate still stands on the Opeongo Road on the outskirts of town. You will recognize it by its high brick gables and treed grounds.

## Renfrew to Dacre

Follow Opeongo Road west from Raglan Street for 6 km to Highway 132 and turn left. After less than 1 km turn left again onto the Opeongo Road, which diverges from Highway 132 here, and drive 2 km to Ferguslea. Founded before the Opeongo Road opened, Ferguslea became a busy stopping place for the roads' settlers. Today its hotels are gone, and the historic hamlet has newer country houses and only a handful of early homes.

Continue through Ferguslea to rejoin Highway 132, and turn left. From this junction to its intersection with Highway 41, about 20 km west, highway widening has buried and bypassed the winding old road, but the landscape is little changed. The terrain is still rugged, the swamps numerous. The few farms along here were small, and today the log barns and weathered houses peer from fields that are overgrown and forgotten.

About 10 km from Ferguslea, just past the junction of Highway 132 and Gorra Hill Road, a small collection of buildings marks the site of another former road village, one with the very Irish name of Shamrock. It too predates the road, settled by a band of Irish who fled Ireland during the deadly potato famines of the 1840s.

About 3 km past Shamrock, turn left onto the Mount St. Patrick Road for a side trip to an interesting church. After about 5 km, the twisting road brings you to Mount St. Patrick. This was the location of the agency for the Opeongo Road, where hopeful settlers would meet the road agent and select their free lots. Today, it is known for its high-steepled stone Roman Catholic church, built

in 1869. It has long been a pilgrimage destination because of its "Holy Well." Irish legends hold that certain springs, or "holy wells," have spiritual powers.

Continue west through Mount St. Patrick and drive to Flat Road and turn right. Here the broad, flat lowland of the Ottawa Valley halts abruptly at the looming form of the Black Donald Mountains—a great granite ridge with peaks that soar more than 300 metres above the lowlands. For 9 km the road winds past the foot of these peaks (now the popular Mount St. Patrick ski area) and through a valley of forests and old farms until it comes back to the Opeongo Road itself and the village of Dacre.

## Dacre

Dacre was once the largest place on the Opeongo, the junction of roads that lead north to Eganville and south to Calabogie, with hotels on all four corners. Sadly, many of its historic hotels and houses have been demolished. But enough remains to give you the feel of a true pioneer landscape. An even more interesting pioneer landscape awaits you about 3 km north, the ghost town of Balaclava. Here, gathered about a weedy millpond at the outlet from Constant Lake, stand a sawmill, a blacksmith's shop and a store, all of which have changed little since the pioneer days, and all now empty.

The rambling wooden mill was originally built by Duncan Ferguson in 1885 and continued to be driven by the water of the creek right up to the late 1960s. Its frame, burner and machinery all remain in place. Sadly, no agency has been able to preserve this unique piece of early Ontario for future generations, and its future is uncertain.

## Dacre to Brudenell

Return to Dacre and continue west on Highway 132. After 2.5 km you will come to an intersection with Highway 41. Turn right and, after 1.5 km, turn left to return to the Opeongo Road.

The Opeongo here is no longer a provincial highway, but rather a municipal road, which, although it has been straightened and asphalted, still retains enough of its pioneer curves and bumps to take you back to the days of pioneer travel. For 10 km it winds along the foot of the lofty Black Donald Mountains. Bordering the road are dense wood-lots and rugged pastures. And there, in the small clearings, one sees pioneer farms with their string barns, a style unique to this region. Unfortunately, many of the log cabins that stood along the road have been bought by land developers and removed to distant sites to become cottages or ski chalets. The Catholic church you pass is all that survives of the pioneer community of Esmonde.

At the first crossroads, on the north side, you will see a rare example of a pioneer homestead. Four attached log barns enclose the small barnyard.

The trail on the south of the road leads you to some real ghosts. High in the mountains lies an abandoned settlement. As the lands along the Opeongo filled, branch roads were pushed into high mountain gulches. There, the soils were at their worst, and many of these side settlements were forsaken. One went by the optimistic name of Newfoundout. If you wish to make a side trip to look at it, turn left from the Opeongo Road at the Davidson farm onto what's left of the road. After 5 km you will see, amid the overgrown fields that have now almost reverted to forest, the collapsing shells of half a dozen log cabins and barns. The rugged terrain defeated the settlement's pioneers. This side trip takes you up the steep mountainside, so it is best attempted in a 4-wheel-drive vehicle or on foot.

The church at Rockingham remains a focus for the community.

Continuing on the Opeongo, the road wanders along the foot of the mountains and into a pocket of relatively productive soil. Here a rural settlement known as Clontarf sprang up and still offers a good collection of period buildings including the St. Clement's Lutheran Church; pioneer farmsteads that still retain their log cabins, barns and outbuildings; and a large white house that was known as Plaunt's Stopping Place, one of the best known of the Opeongo's hotels.

Now the road begins its long climb to the summit of McDonald's Mountain. As you grind slowly up the hill, the roadside drops away. Below

Lonely log barns litter the fields of Newfoundout.

you shimmer the waters of Lake Clear. Beyond the lake the fields and forests of the Ottawa Valley roll into the distance until they reach the Gatineau Hills of Quebec, 70 km away. Geologists will tell you that the Ottawa Valley is a huge block of rock that cracked away from the adjacent rock and sank. The Gatineaus and the Black Donalds are the rocks that held firm. The land between them is still sinking today. You may hear your Ottawa friends tell of occasional earthquakes. This is the reason.

For the next 10 km, the road rollercoasters over the lofty peaks. Even here, pioneers tried to wrest their fortunes from the rocky ground. Again, many of the log buildings still stand. One of those is the Vanbrugh School, among the few log schoolhouses in Ontario still on its original site and now a private residence.

Just past the school you come to a T intersection with Highway 512. Turn left and, after 1 km you will come to a startlingly modern town, Foymount. Built after the Second World War, this was a radar base and townsite. Modern homes, apartments, and even a recreational hall and library were built on curving, suburban-like streets. But the base has long since closed, and its radar domes dismantled. Efforts to revive the site have been only partially successful and many of the apartments and buildings sit empty, the lawns overgrown.

From Foymount, continue west on Highway 512 as the Opeongo Road swings back from the crest of the mountains to wind over the highland plateau. Although lofty rock outcroppings still peer down, the pockets of soil between them are wider

Opposite: The residents of Wilno proudly celebrate their Polish heritage.

Barry's Bay's Booth Line railway station and water tank have both been preserved.

and deeper; the fields are larger and the farms more numerous. Then, 10 km from Foymount, you will come to the town of Brudenell, almost a ghost town.

## Brudenell

Like Dacre, Brudenell marked the junction of two colonization roads, the Opeongo and the Peterson, and was one of the larger villages on either road. Most of its stores, hotels and houses are gone now. The only vestiges of its pioneer legacy are the former Costello Hotel on the south side of the road, and the nearby former store.

At Brudenell, Highway 512 follows the Peterson Road north. But your route continues straight along the Opeongo. A few kilometers beyond the intersection is Our Lady of the Angels Roman Catholic Church, built using red stone. Beyond

the church and on the left, the Letterkenny Road leads to Rockingham, another interesting old pioneer site.

## Side Trip to Rockingham

If you wish to make a side trip to this pioneer village, follow the Letterkenny Road for 4 km and then turn right onto the Rockingham Road. After a further 2 km the road descends into the gully of Rockingham Creek.

Rockingham sits nestled in this wooded hollow, its rustic pioneer buildings little changed and its simple wooden church the oldest on the trip. Rockingham dates from 1859, when John Watson led a band of English colonists to a mill site on the Peterson Road. The village grew quickly and soon added a gristmill, a sawmill, several stores, taverns and hotels, and St. Leonard's Church. Many of these structures remain, including the church. It was one of the few built using a board-and-batten style. Fortunately, thanks to local efforts, it survives.

## Brudenell to Barry's Bay

Return to the Opeongo Road and continue west, where the road enters its most truly pioneer state. For the next 10 km the terrain is rugged, the farms few. Some of the old farmsteads retain their early log barns, a few their log homes. A short distance past Hopefield Road, County Road 66 leads north. Continue straight ahead to remain on the Opeongo. Here, too, the road becomes narrower, the curves and hills steeper. But all too soon the Opeongo emerges from its pioneer past and stops at Highway 60. Only 3 km to the left lies Barry's Bay, a lakeside lumber town and the heart of Canada's first Polish community.

Since Barry's Bay had more locational advantages than the other towns of the Opeongo Road, it grew larger and stayed that way. Its position on Kamaniskeg Lake meant that logs could be boated in from much of the extensive Madawaska River watershed, an area particularly rich in pine. When John Rudolphus Booth, Canada's premier 19th-century lumber magnate, added his railway in the 1890s, it boomed even larger.

During this period, the Poles began to arrive. Between 1864 and 1895, more than 300 Poles migrated to Canada to settle the Opeongo Road and nearby lands. But the harsh conditions caused many of them to give up farming, and they moved to Barry's Bay and to Wilno, a nearby village, where they engaged in lumbering. Wilno is named after a town in Poland and, although smaller than Barry's Bay, remains the cultural focus of the Polish community. The village, with its twin-spired cathedral, stands 8 km east on Highway 60. Stop into the Wilno Tavern for some genuine Polish cuisine such as sledzie (pickled herring), golabki (cabbage rolls) or pierogies.

Many buildings in Barry's Bay date from its lumber days. Look in particular for the Balmoral Hotel, an early lumberman's hotel and now a popular family restaurant. Opposite the hotel, the Barry's Bay railway station is now a museum. This building is the oldest Booth station still standing, a rare find especially with its rare wooden water tank still standing nearby.

After your long drive through pioneer country, you will appreciate the town's other features. Set at the junction of two modern provincial highways, 60 and 62, Barry's Bay caters to the travelling public and has a selection of stores, restaurants and picnic facilities.

To return home, Highway 60 leads east toward Ottawa or west through Algonquin Park to Highway 11. Highway 62 leads south to the Belleville area. But you won't be in a rush to leave, for the ghosts of the Opeongo pioneers will beckon you to linger.

# 17 The Remarkable Highlands of Hastings

Between Toronto and Ottawa, in the northern part of a county called Hastings, there is a remote region of mountain scenery that is unmatched elsewhere in southern Ontario. This backroads trip takes you through the area on a circular route that begins in Bancroft and follows a series of mountain roads for about 80 km. The beauty of the hills is a naturalist's delight, while the many pioneer homes, barns and general stores offer much for the photographer and historian alike.

This is a tour that will appeal to the rockhounds as well, since the hills around Bancroft have become internationally known for their minerals and their gemstones. Each summer, during Bancroft's Gemboree, rockhounds arrive from throughout North America to scour them.

Although the route has no facilities other than general stores (and even they are few), you will never be more than half an hour's drive from Bancroft, where there are restaurants, motels and a full range of services. If you are coming from the Toronto area, you can reach Bancroft via Highways 401, 35/115 and 28. From Ottawa follow Highway 7 to Highway 62, which leads north to Bancroft.

Although two good provincial highways bisect the area, the Highlands of Hastings retains the feel of its pioneering roots. Bancroft has only 3,800 residents, and its nearest neighbour of comparable size, Madoc, is more than 70 km away. The highlands themselves are a high rugged plateau deep in the Canadian Shield, surrounded by the canyons of the Madawaska, Mississippi and York Rivers.

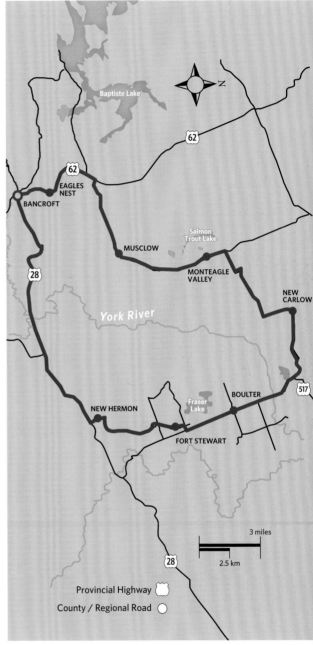

- - - - - - - - - - - - - - - - - - - - - - - - - - - - -

**Opposite: The view from the lookout near Bancroft encompasses the valley of the York River.**

Although the area was not railway country, Bancroft has preserved its historic station.

Settlement came late to north Hastings, and with good reason. Although loggers had swept up the Madawaska Valley and decimated much of the area's forests during the early decades of the 19th century, settlers had been discouraged by the poor access, the swamps and the forbidding rocky highlands. Finally in the 1850s and 1860s, the government held out the twin carrots of new roads and free land, and pioneer farmers at last began to arrive.

The first of the colonization roads, the Hastings, was built northward from Madoc in 1855 and finished by about 1860. Soon, other branch roads were opened, including the Mississippi Road to the old Perth settlement in the east; the Monck Road to the west; and across the north, the Peterson Road.

The site that would be Bancroft had an advantage from the very beginning. Not only was it the junction of the Hastings and the Monck colonization roads, but it possessed excellent water power—a steep falls on the York River. As Bancroft boomed as a lumber town, the hills began to fill with settlers. But when the trees disappeared, so did the lumbermen. However, the area had one more natural resource that would help retain its prosperity—its minerals. In the rocks lay a remarkable variety of minerals. While they lacked the glamour of gold and silver, the minerals served a variety of industrial uses. There was feldspar, mica and corundum, the hardest mineral then known, and, of course, uranium. Although the mines are closed now, the abundance of collectible minerals and the beauty of the highlands have brought new life through tourism and an active arts community.

Opposite: Egan Chutes Provincial Park.

## Bancroft

Bancroft began in 1879, when the Bronson Lumber company moved its headquarters to the falls on the York River. Mills, churches and hotels quickly sprang up by the mills and around the intersection of the two settlement roads. Then, in 1900, the Central Ontario Railway rumbled into town, followed in 1903 by the Irondale, Bancroft and Ottawa Railway.

Although many of the original stores have been replaced or been covered with plastic and plate glass, Bancroft retains a frontier appearance. One of the town's most attractive and historic buildings is the Bancroft Hotel, built in 1899, which now houses TO's Pub and Thomas Oliver's Restaurant. On Railway Street, one block north, is the preserved COR railway station, repainted from CNR red to its original colours of red and white. It has housed an art gallery, a mineral museum and community services. You will also find on the site a log cabin built for the Bronson Company in 1853 and moved to town as a Centennial project in 1967.

## Bancroft to New Hermon

Before leaving Bancroft, obtain a rockhound's guide from the Chamber of Commerce listing 30 of the more interesting rock-collecting sites. Then leave Bancroft east on Highway 28, which closely follows the route of the Mississippi Colonization Road. After 3 km, look for the Princess Sodalite Mine. A rare, decorative blue stone, sodalite is found in only a few locations throughout the world. This once busy mine is now a rock shop with a "rock farm" that has nearly 100 specimens of minerals.

## Rockhounds' Side Trip #1

Continue east for another 4 km to the York River and the Egan Chutes Provincial Park. Although the park is not signed, dirt roads lead north from each side of the bridge over the river. In the old quarries along these trails lie samples of chondronite, spinal and wollastonite, and possibly even small quantities of sodalite. The Chamber of Commerce booklet gives you the details. Trails lead farther along the river to the falls themselves.

Your main route continues east along Highway 28. As you emerge from the York River Valley, you will see the foothills of the Black Donald Mountains looming ahead. A drive of 8 km brings you into these foothills and to the junction of the Fort Stewart Road (originally known as the New Carlow Road), which was built to link the Peterson Colonization Road in the north with the Mississippi Road. At its original junction with the old Mississippi Road (a little to the south of today's Highway 28) was the village of Hermon, which has long since vanished. But its successor, New Hermon, still exists, only a couple of kilometres north. Drive north from Highway 28, and almost immediately you will come to New Hermon's homes.

## New Hermon to New Carlow

Keep right at the fork in New Hermon and continue north on Fort Stewart Road as it twists its way into the hills, passing scattered clearings of pioneer farms. After 5 km it, arrives at the breezy summit of a high plateau and the hamlet of Fort Stewart. This settlement was an early stopping place on the road, and its hotels provided rest and nourishment for weary stagecoach travellers. The Stewart part of its name derives from an early hotelkeeper; the "Fort," from the height of land the hamlet occupies. Although the hotels are gone, the village still contains several early buildings.

From Fort Stewart, continue north for 1 km to a T intersection at Whytes Road. Turn right, and, after half a kilometre, you will come to a view worth lingering over. Here, the plateau plunges 100 metres into the valley of the Little Mississippi

Ontario has some surprisingly mountainous scenery hidden along this backroad.

River, while beyond the valley the forested peaks of the Black Donald Mountains roll toward the horizon.

Turn left at the intersection and continue on Boulter Road, which follows the top of the plateau for 5 km. The northern peak of the plateau is crowned by the village of Boulter, which was named after an early county warden. Boulter began as a roadside stopping place for travellers and developed into a farm service village. North of Boulter, the scenery shifts dramatically once more. As the York River Valley opens at your feet, the road glides down the slope of the plateau and into a swampy lowland. Here it crosses over the York River, which meanders northeastward to the mighty Madawaska.

About 1.5 km north of the bridge, look for Park Road to the left. This short lane leads to Fosters Lake, one of the few lakes that are tucked into

these highlands, and to one of the area's few municipal roads with a beach and picnic ground. If you have packed a lunch, this is the place to have it, for there are no other lakeside parks on this route.

Near this turnoff, look for Highway 517 leading northeast. This offers you a side trip to Craigmont, once one of the world's leading corundum producers and now a ghost town (only a few overgrown foundations and village streets remain) and rockhound site. It is about 6 km along and down the Craigmont Road to the east.

As you continue north from the park, your route bends westward to complete half of the circle.

## Rockhounds' Side Trip #2

Rockhounds should, after 2 km, look for a dirt road on the right. It leads to the site of the once busy Burgess mines, another corundum operation. After 1.1 km, it will bring you to a hunting

The road passes through the rugged rural hamlet of New Carlow.

lodge located roughly on the site of the old village. On the hill behind it, in the old pits, you may find some crystals of corundum. But be sure to take a pick and hammer, for corundum is one of the world's hardest minerals. Park well beyond the lodge and remember that the owners' facilities are off limits to rockhounds.

Back on the Boulter Road, after 3 km you will come to a T intersection. Here is the picturesque hamlet of New Carlow, which was once a busy crossroads village. Its store, school and shops are closed now, but many of the buildings still cluster about the intersection and dot the wooded hillside over Papineau Creek.

## New Carlow to Musclow

Turn left onto New Carlow Road and cross the bridge over Papineau Creek. The road now climbs out of the valley and onto another mountaintop plateau. Here, again, the level and relatively fertile soils have sustained a small farming community. At the second intersection the road bends right and descends into a dark, swampy valley, then mounts yet another plateau, which has the curious name of Monteagle Valley (Monteagle being an English lord). Here you come to a T intersection with East Road Loop, where you should turn left. As you drive south from the intersection, look to the left for views across the valley of the York River to the plateaus and mountains through which you have just travelled. Here the landscape changes once more as the road twists through the rugged foothills and descends through a chain of ravines to the flat sand plains that lie north of Bancroft.

At 4 km from your last turn, the road meets another T intersection. Turn left here onto the

Musclow-Greenview Road. Throughout this area, the mountainsides have been dissected by the rivers and creeks that are slowly eroding their way into the plateau.

## Rockhounds' Side Trip #3

Shortly after the turn, look for the MacDonald Mine Road leading to the right. Drive for 3.6 km to an open area on the right. A 200 metre walk will bring you to the old mine site where you can rummage in the piles for feldspar, quartz and pyrite (fool's gold). (At the time of writing, summer of 2012, the site was unavailable to visitors.)

Your original route stays on the Musclow-Greenview Road and brings you to the historic hamlet of Musclow, which took its name from a pioneer family. Musclow began life as a busy service village at a once important road junction, but it ceased to serve this purpose when the road that led east to Fort Stewart was closed. Still, a few of the old village buildings yet guard the intersection. Many of the old pioneer farmsteads in this area provide prime subject material for the landscape photographer.

Keep right in the village corner and follow the Musclow-Greenview Road west for another 6 km. This road descends from the plateau through forested ravines and emerges onto a wide sandy plain. Here, at Highway 62, the mountain road ends. You have come almost full circle and are 7 km north of Bancroft.

This side trip leads to a high lookout. Turn left onto Highway 62 from the Musclow-Greenview Road, drive for 3.5 km and then follow the signs to the Eagle's Nest Park. From this vantage point, the wide valley of the York River opens at your feet. The cliff itself is an outlier of the plateau from which you have just descended. Looking north, you can easily discern the high plateau wall as it winds its way along the York Valley.

**A view of the MacDonald Mine.**

As you can see along Highway 62, many of Ontario's historic landscapes have vanished, buried by the relentless demand for roadside commercial sprawl, and even here there are big box stores. However the distance from the heaviest urban growth has saved much of the region's heritage, at least for the time being.

Nipissing

534

522

Commanda

Sundridge

Magnetawan

124

18

69

11

Parry
Sound

Orrville

Georgian
Bay

Huntsville

60

Rosseau

141

69

Elliot
Lake

17

108

Espanola

Blind River

6

North Channel

540

Little
Current

Gore Bay

Kagawong

Meldrum
Bay

19

West Bay

Silver
Water

Evansville

542

Lake
Huron

Manitoulin
Island

South Baymouth

11

65

New
Liskeard

11b

11

20

Cobalt

North
Cobalt

Silver Centre

Lake Timiskaming

101

QUEBEC

N

# Section 4
# Northern Ontario

# 18 The Nipissing: A Road of Broken Dreams

from forest to farms. In 1925 the area's first hydro-electric plant whirred into life, powered by the falls in the river. Although commercial traffic on the canal ceased in the early 1950s, and the hydro plant fell silent soon after, Magnetawan continued to prosper.

The old plant, with its original generators still in place, is now a museum. It stands a few paces east of the Nipissing Road on Highway 510. The picturesque town invites you to linger, whether at the historic Schmeler Hotel, in one of the family restaurants or simply beside the waters of the river.

## Magnetawan to Commanda

Leave Magnetawan north on Highways 520 and 510, which is the Nipissing Road alignment. Then, after 4 km, cross Highway 124 to stay on the Nipissing Road. Here, once more, the road is as the pioneer travellers might remember it. The forest is dark, as the route bends and twists around each obstacle. There are few clearings here and no old cabins. So dreadful was the soil that settlers shunned this area completely. Past the Youthdale Road, the Nipissing Road is no longer passable. If driving, you will need to return to Highway 124 and drive east to Pearceley Road and follow it north to Centre Road, where you turn left to get back to the Nipissing Road alignment.

After 18 km, there appears a clearing and a white frame house. This is the site of a one-time village, Mecunoma, and its famous hotel with the colourful name of Bummers' Roost. The original hotel burned in 1926, and today's house was built on the hotel foundations. This brings you to a T intersection with the Eagle Lake Road. Beyond the intersection, the Nipissing Road is no longer suitable for vehicles—so you should turn right

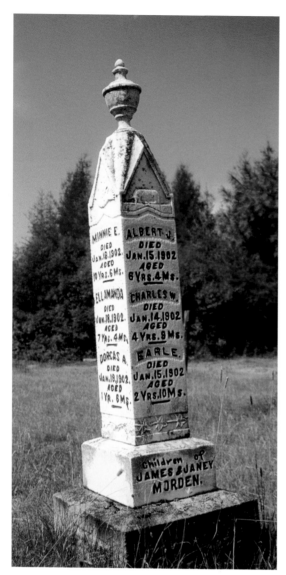

Cemeteries often tell tales of harsh, even deadly, conditions along the Nipissing Road.

historical plaque commemorates the story of the Nipissing Road.

Situated at the junction of the Nipissing Road, the Ahmic Road and the Magnetawan Canal, Magnetawan grew quickly during the 19th century. Settlers, many of them Swiss, crammed the steamers from Burks Falls and turned the valley

Opposite: A typical schoolhouse in a forest setting found on Ontario's pioneer roads.

on Eagle Lake Road and follow it for 1.5 km to the Rye Road, where you go left. After 2 km on this road, you will rejoin the original alignment of the Nipissing at the abandoned hamlet of Rye. Gone now are the store, post office and log hotels—some sources say there were as many as four hotels—and Rye today consists of a collapsing school and a cemetery.

An intersection 1.5 km north of the school marks the centre of the vanished hamlet. The white frame church was demolished in the mid-1980s, but the cemetery contains a number of white wooden crosses beside the headstones where many of the family names reflect the Germanic origins of the early pioneers.

As you travel north from this quiet intersection, you will pass the remains of a series of former bush farms, until the original road once more becomes impassable.

If using an ATV or a dirt bike, follow the Rye Road to Jerusalem Road that leads to the right and go 6 km to a T intersection. Turn left and continue for 3 km to another T intersection. Here you pass through the abandoned and long-vanished settlement of Mandeville. The land is low and swampy, and a young forest closes in overhead. At this intersection, turn left again. Once more you emerge onto a rocky upland; the hills, however, are steeper. After winding through a mature forest and past more old farms, keep right on the Rye Road to Highway 522 and turn left to Commanda, where you once more encounter the Nipissing Road. Please note that this portion is not passable for regular vehicles.

## Commanda to Nipissing

Named for a local Ojibwa chief, Commanda is a small cluster of houses. Here, in 1885, James Arthur built the area's first general store. It was larger than most for a pioneer village—two storeys high, with a double porch and extensions to each side. Arthur distinguished his store with elaborate flourishes to its fretwork. Although most such buildings would have been replaced or severely altered, the Commanda store has survived five ownerships intact. Then, in 1980, the Gurd Township and Area Historical Corporation purchased the building and refurbished it as a turn-of-the-century general

The old general store in Commanda is now a unique general store museum.

Manitoulin Island is the world's largest freshwater island—120 km in length, though it narrows in places to just 2 km in width. It has more than 20 inland lakes and one of Ontario's longest dead-end highways. Highway 540, which is the backroad for this trip, is 100 km long and follows the cliffs and coves from Little Current at the island's eastern end to Manitoulin's western tip.

Despite its size, Manitoulin has no traditional road access. There are indeed only two approaches for drivers bound for Manitoulin Island. One is via Highway 6 south from the Trans-Canada Highway 17, 70 km west of Sudbury. This is a route noted for its high, scenic passes across the La Cloche Mountains, a rugged ridge of white quartzite. The access to the island, however, is not by a normal highway bridge, but rather by a paved and decommissioned CPR railway bridge.

The other approach is over the water. Ontario's largest car ferry, the *Chi-Cheemaun*, offers three daily sailings during the summer between Tobermory, at the tip of the Bruce Peninsula, and South Baymouth, on Highway 6, 65 km south of Little Current. Translated from the Ojibwa, the ferry's name means "Big Canoe."

Here is a territory that mainstream Ontario has only lately discovered. Despite proposals for mega developments, there remains a legacy of vanished sawmills and abandoned farmsteads. Many of the villages and towns have changed little since Manitoulin's boom period of the late 1880s, and they provide rustic subject material for photographers. High on Manitoulin's cliffs you will find hiking trails, lookouts and picnic tables, and, in their shadow, inland lakes for fishing, boating or swimming.

**Opposite: A former railway swing bridge remains the only road access to the world's largest freshwater island.**

Centuries ago, Manitoulin was a Native stronghold that its aboriginal inhabitants, the Ottawa, called Ekantoten. However, during the 17th century, the Iroquois incursions forced the Ottawa to flee to the shores of Lake Michigan, where they remained until 1836. In that year, the lieutenant-governor of Upper Canada, Sir Francis Bond Head, selected the large island as the centre of Native relocations. The scattered tribes returned, reluctantly at first, but by 1860 more than 1,300 Ottawa and Ojibwa were occupying a cluster of towns at the east end of the island.

But the haven was short-lived. Bowing to pressure from lumbermen and settlers, the Indian Branch sent William Bartlett and Charles Lindsay to take back the island. The Native peoples in return were to receive a paltry 10 hectares each. Not surprisingly, they refused. The strongest opposition came from the large contingent who occupied the Wikwemikong Peninsula. The next year William McDougall, commissioner of Crown lands, tried again, but he too was rebuffed. Only when he arbitrarily excluded the Wikwemikong from voting about ceding their lands did the other, smaller bands relent and move reluctantly to reserves. The Wikwemikongs, however, never yielded their lands, and today the Wikwemikong Peninsula remains Ontario's only unceded First Nations territory.

Then, between 1864 and 1879, the surveyors moved in, and by 1882 the government had sold 120,000 hectares, much of it to absentee speculators who resold it at several times its original price.

The first European settlements appeared in sheltered coves. By 1881, fishermen and lumbermen had set up mills and fishing stations in Little Current, Honora, Kagawong, Gore Bay, Cooks Dock and Michaels Bay. Early life was hard, and the tough berry, the haw berry, became a staple of the pioneer diet, so much so that the island's early farmers nicknamed each other the "haweaters." The name has survived to this day and now is used to promote tourism.

At first, only two roads linked the settlements: colonization trails from Michaels Bay, the island's first main port of entry on the south coast to Manitowaning, and to Gore Bay. But by the turn of century, farm concession roads had opened throughout the island, and the old pioneer trails were in parts completely abandoned while Michaels Bay itself became a ghost town.

Farming, fishing and forestry developed as mainstays for the island's economy, but each soon declined. Fire and overcutting combined to sweep the forests clean. Overfishing and the dreaded predator, the sea lamprey, defeated the fishery. And the stony and infertile soils that should never have been cultivated in the first place drove away most of the farmers. Since 1900, Manitoulin's population has risen from 10,000 to 13,000. The spectre of large development looms, and major projects now threaten the island's serenity.

Nevertheless, the picturesque vestiges of early settlement and the natural beauty of the cliffs and waters combine to make the Haweater Trail a wonderful way to explore the island.

## Little Current

Manitoulin, the world's largest freshwater island, has the most unusual form of road access, an abandoned railway bridge. Built by the Algoma Eastern Railway, the Canadian Pacific Railway's predecessor, the bridge has been paved to allow autos. During navigation season it swings open for 10 minutes each hour to allow boats to pass.

The bridge leads to the island's main community, Little Current. From the south the highway enters Little Current on Manitowaning Road, an early colonization road. The town's main business district lines the shore on Water Street, where you

**Kagawong is one of the route's most picturesque villages.**

can watch the sleek American yachts glide to dockside, fresh from a battle with the turbulent North Channel. Along the street are grocery stores, gift shops, the popular Anchor Inn tavern and offices of the *Manitoulin Expositor*, a community newspaper that has been published since 1879.

## Little Current to Kagawong

The mighty rock ridge known as the Niagara Escarpment dips beneath the waters of Georgian Bay at the northern tip of the Bruce Peninsula and re-emerges to form the backbone of Manitoulin Island. The escarpment's cliffs form the island's north shore, ring its fjord-like bays and loom over its flat plains.

The first section of your trip follows the base of the escarpment and leads you to its highest lookouts and through its early ports. Your first lookout point, and one of the highest, lies close to Little Current. Follow Highway 6 south to 10 Mile Point lookout with ample parking and a gift shop (complete with haw berry jelly). Views here extend northward over the various channels that separate the island from the mainland, and to the gleaming white La Cloche Mountains. Return to Little Current and follow Highway 540 west. Here, old farms mix with newer country homes until, after 2 km, the road enters the Sucker Creek First Nation territory. After 3 km, the road leaves the territory, traverses another small farming community and then meets the shoreline. For the next 6 km it follows the shoreline though, for most of this stretch, trees block the view. The road then bends south to Honora, where a handful of homes are all that remain of a once busy fishing and sawmilling port.

At 6 km south of Honora, Highway 540 meets the Bidwell Road and your access to the Cup and Saucer Trail, a hiking trail to the island's highest lookout point. The Cup and Saucer (named for its appearance) is a rock formation that looms high above the road. The trail is about 2 km long and includes steps and rails to help you up the steeper portions. The views from the top are panoramic. Below, to the east, lie the waters of Lake Manitou, and beyond that the farmlands of the eastern end of the island. To the west lie West Bay and the North Channel of Lake Huron. Allow about three hours for the hike.

Continuing west from the trail, the road brings you to the First Nation village of M'Chigeeng, the site of an early Native Canadian settlement called Mechocowedong. It is the island's most populous Native territory (Wikwemikong is the largest geographically) and, with its three art galleries, is one of Ontario's more important centres for First Nations artists. You can find their works in the Ojibwe Cultural Foundation, which you enter through a piece of stone artwork called "Bringing the Family Together." Across the road, the Immaculate Conception Church's architecture is meant to symbolize a tepee. Here, too, you will find galleries, craft shops and restaurants. Take a look especially at Lillian's Porcupine Quill Basket Museum.

West of M'Chigeeng, Highway 540 swings inland for about 3 km and then turns straight north to cross a small agricultural plain. After 4 km, it bends west to the historic and picturesque village of Kagawong.

## Kagawong

Kagawong lies about 1 km north of the highway on the shores of Mudge Bay. Like most of the island's cove villages, Kagawong began as a milling, fishing and shipping centre, but it had one more feature that the others lacked—water power. Just

2 km inland lies Lake Kagawong, from which a small river drains northward to the lip of a deep gorge. The 20 metre drop in the river powered early sawmills and later an electric powerhouse. Today it provides the focus for a small park beside the highway.

The village, a string of buildings along the road by the bay, contains some of the island's most appealing architecture. Here stand a former pulp mill, now the Old Mill Heritage Centre Museum, a store and a hotel all dating from the 1890s when the village was rebuilt following a fire. The Anglican church contains a pulpit made from the wreck of an old ship, while its stained-glass windows depict a ship and anchor. You can take a walking tour of the village; or you can continue your drive out to Maple Point and a scenic panorama of the North Channel Islands.

## Kagawong to Gore Bay

From Kagawong, Highway 540 crosses a limestone plain to the island's first major town, and one of its most picturesque, Gore Bay. Gore Bay was once larger than Little Current, its future more promising. Today it has slid to second place. To enter Gore Bay, turn right from Highway 540 onto Highway 542 and drive 2 km into the town.

## Gore Bay

One of Manitoulin's first European settlements, Gore Bay was the terminus of a colonization road from Michaels Bay on the south shore. By 1895 it had become not just a fishing and shipping port, but the centre of a prosperous farming community and the seat of the district court. Only a few buildings date from its early days, because in 1908 a fire razed most of the business district.

As Highway 542 enters the town it becomes Meredith Street, the business street where you will find most of the stores. Two blocks away on Phipps

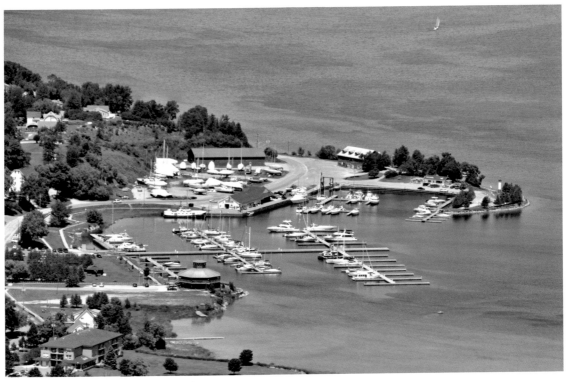

Gore Bay is a popular destination for boaters and tourists during the summer months.

Street is the 1889 courthouse, which somehow escaped the flames. Beside it stands the jail built in 1895, which now houses the museum. Here you can look at a turn-of-the-century cell, as well as at early telephones and dental equipment.

Down on the water, you can visit the new tourist pavilion with its art gallery and tea room. Before leaving, drive out along East Bluff Road, or take West Bluff Road to Janet Head Park. Either route will reward you with sweeping vistas of the cliff-lined harbour and the wind-tossed waters of the North Channel.

## Gore Bay to Silver Water

This section of the route traverses one of the island's most fertile plains, crosses a long cause-way, and includes watery lookouts and a pair of ghost ports.

Continue west from Gore Bay on Highway 540. For 4.5 km, the road crosses fertile farming plains. Here you will pass some modern farms, their fields wide and green, herds of beef cattle lazily grazing. As Highway 540 bends sharply south, Highway 540A leads to the island township of Barrie Island, a low limestone plateau with two dozen farms. But keep on Highway 540 and follow it south toward Lake Wolsey.

The road continues through farm country for about 4 km and then enters the narrow peninsula that divides Bayfield Sound, a wide indentation of the North Channel, from Lake Wolsey. This 2 km long peninsula is separated from the south shore of the lake by a 1 km wide channel, which Highway 540 crosses on a scenic causeway. Off to the side is a roadside park that offers picnic facilities and a chance to fish. The south end of Lake Wolsey, which lies only 2 km from Manitoulin's south shore, marks the narrowest point of the island. Before crossing you can pause at Indian Point Bridge lookout to enjoy the view.

Continuing west on Highway 540 you pass through the communities of Evansville and Elizabeth Bay before arriving in the village of Silver Water.

## Silver Water

Silver Water was once western Manitoulin's most important village, the retail centre for a busy farming area and for two ports. But the ports have vanished, along with their fishermen, sawmills and cabins, and many farms are now abandoned. Their decline affected the village and many of its original buildings are now gone. A few new homes have been added along with a newer general store.

If you are a history enthusiast, you may want to visit the vanished port of Cooks Dock. Tucked beneath a 100 metre cliff, it was at the turn of the century a fishing station and a lumber shipping port. To reach it, turn right on Cooks Dock Road and drive 5 km to the dock site. No buildings have survived from the shipping and fishing days, but if you search the bush you may recover an old bottle or kettle.

## Silver Water to Meldrum Bay

This, the last segment of the route, passes isolated pockets of farmlands, ventures into a tiny village of white houses on a green hillside, and ends at a curious lighthouse museum. It is as far as you go on Manitoulin.

From Silver Water, continue west on Highway 540. For 28 km the road traverses a rugged land of rock and forest. Overgrown clearings tell of futile farming efforts. Then on the right, as the road makes a sharp swing left, the blue waters of Meldrum Bay sparkle between the trees. A

kilometre beyond that lies the village of Meldrum Bay. The bay from which the village derived its name is ringed with steep, forested hills. On the western shore are the church, hotel, stores and houses. Today, Meldrum Bay is home to only about 160 permanent residents, but at the turn of the century it contained a sawmill and a colony of fishermen. Now only the mill's foundations remain.

The community sees little traffic, and the pace is leisurely. Here you can visit the Meldrum Bay Country Store or enjoy a meal (or overnight stay) at the century-old Meldrum Bay Inn. And don't leave out the Net Shed Museum, a former net storage shed that is operated by the small but active Meldrum Bay Historical Society. It is open daily on alternating mornings and afternoons throughout the summer months and displays early photographs and fishing equipment.

The ambience of the place is to be enjoyed. Where else can you find yourself at the end of a 100 km long dead-end road? The tranquility and the maritime legacy combine to transport you back in time.

## Meldrum Bay to Mississagi Lighthouse

From the village, rejoin Highway 540 for 1 km to a side road where a directional arrow points to the lighthouse. The dirt road crosses Manitoulin's most remote farming community and then, after 3 km, narrows and becomes a more rugged trail, twisting through the bush. After 5 km it emerges into a small, rocky clearing. Ahead stands the Mississagi Lighthouse. En route it will be hard to miss the Lafarge dolomite quarry, one of Ontario's largest, which ships their product on large ocean-going freighters.

Built before the turn of the 19th century to guide ships along the channel between Manitoulin and Cockburn Islands, the lighthouse is now a

The Mississagi Lighthouse is now a museum and campground office.

museum. It is a squat wooden structure, painted the mandatory red and white. The attached keeper's cabin is furnished in a turn-of-the-century style and contains equipment that the keeper of the period used. The Mississagi Lighthouse tops a low limestone bluff, the crest of the Niagara Escarpment, just before it dips once more beneath Lake Huron's chilly waters.

From the light level, you can view the rocky shoreline below you and the distant form of the ghost island of Cockburn Island. There the main village of Tolsmaville is now a seasonal community. Its former concession roads have three dozen farms, all vacant, which tell of a once-bustling island community of farmers, fishermen and loggers who were forced to leave when the vital steamer service that linked them with the outside world was discontinued.

Overleaf: Sunset over Manitoulin Island.

# 20 Boomtown Backroads: The Cobalt Circle

More than ten years ago, a TV Ontario panel of historians (this author included) awarded Cobalt the designation, "Ontario's Most Historic Town"—and there was a reason for that. It was the silver discovery here in 1903 that spawned a world-famous silver rush creating a boomtown and giving the impetus for a railway and the opening of Ontario's northeast. This route explores that heritage, from the boomtown buildings in this unusual town to the skeletal remains of mine headframes that lurk amid the harsh rock knobs surrounding

A headframe marks the entrance into Cobalt.

Cobalt. Thanks to the Cobalt Mining Museum, informative published walking and driving tours will lead the way.

n 1890, northeastern Ontario was touted for its farmland. From the north end of Lake Timiskaming, a flat plain of fine clays, the result of an ancient postglacial lake deposit spreads northwestward. The government of the day heavily promoted the area, which it dubbed the Clay Belt. With only steamers to get them there, settlers docked at places such as New Liskeard and Haileybury, still thriving communities today, and at other places that have vanished, like Hilliardtown and Tomstown.

To make colonization more attractive, the government laid plans to build a colonization railway to carry the settlers. In 1903, while scouting the woods for timber that the railway could use as ties, scouts James McKinley and Ernest Darragh found a dull grey rock that was inordinately heavy. Their discovery, by the shore of Long Lake (now Cobalt Lake), was silver. The rush was on.

Within just five years, more than 100 mines were clanging in the hills around the lake, while on the rocky shore boomed the town of Cobalt. The population grew quickly to 10,000, as simple cabins and gangly stores fought for valuable space on the steep hillsides. Despite local prohibition, Cobalt miners could be sure of satisfying their thirst at illegal booze cans called Blind Pigs. Little wonder that one of its heritage buildings is the Ontario Provincial Police's first lock-up. As prospectors wandered the hills, they uncovered more deposits. By 1909 Cobalt had a rival more than 40 km away, at Silver Centre.

But the small deposits of silver were soon exhausted. Later, as prices for silver plunged, the mines began to close, and by 1940 Cobalt's population had dwindled to fewer than 2,000. Silver Centre was abandoned completely, and it is now a ghost town.

Cobalt retains much of its boomtown appearance.

## Cobalt

By exploring Cobalt and its mining heritage, you will easily understand why TV Ontario's *Studio Two* program labelled Cobalt as "Ontario's Most Historic Town," a deserved designation of which the town's citizens are justly proud. With its twisting sidewalks, old wooden houses and early stores, Cobalt still looks like a boomtown. Although fires and demolitions have taken a heavy toll on its wonderful old buildings, enough remain that you can wander the streets and relive those glory days.

Start at the mining museum on Silver Street. It is one of North America's most celebrated mining museums, containing rare mining equipment, books on the romance of the rush, and Canada's largest collection of silver ore. It occupies the first office of the *Cobalt Nugget*, which during the peak of the boom had avid readers as far away as England and California. In the museum be sure to purchase the Heritage Silver Trail guide and the Cobalt Walking Trail Guide, both excellent.

Beside the museum is the present town hall, in the former YMCA building. Nearby gift and craft shops have moved into the old structures, while on the opposite side of the street is an old-time barber shop. While you're on Silver Street, check the schedule of the Classic Theatre. Built in 1920, the Classic was restored as a theatre in 1995.

Across from the museum, on the Willet Green Miller Memorial site, stands a headframe that was originally located in North Cobalt. The Pan Silver headframe was moved here in 1998 to house the Cobalt Historical Society. An outdoor heritage exhibit displays mining equipment and renderings depicting the town's heritage.

Behind the display and down by the tracks is the magnificent TNO railway station. Built to replace the TNO's original pattern-book station in 1908, the station contained a vaulted two-storey waiting room. After sitting empty for several years, it has been preserved and now is home to the town's welcome centre.

A few paces north of the museum, at the corner of Prospect and Silver Streets, is Cobalt's most unusual group of buildings. On the northeast corner is the Bank of Ottawa building, while on the northwest corner is a former grocery store. What makes this store so unusual is that it has a headframe sticking out of its roof. Anthony Giachino, who built it in 1926, decided to recycle the cool air from the depths of the then abandoned Coniagas mine shaft to cool his meat and vegetables.

On the southwest corner stands the Fraser Hotel, originally the Royal Exchange Building. The Bunker Museum moved here from its earlier home in the train station. Although massive compared with its neighbours today, several equally grand buildings once lined both Prospect and Lang Streets. Lang Street was once described as northern Ontario's premier shopping street with shops extending for more than 1 km. As a result of fires and demolitions, few remain. Prospect Street demonstrates the difficulty in town-building: it ends at a steep flight of stairs that leads to Cobalt Street, where many early homes reflect the boomtown style of housing, as do various other small back streets.

Farther east on Lang Street you come to the old town "square" and a historic grouping of buildings. As you near the new library you will find the firefighters' museum with a wall mural that shows you what Lang Street looked like in its glory days.

## The Heritage Silver Trail

After you have followed the mining museum's walking tour, get back in the car to follow the Heritage Silver Trail guide for a circular tour through the barren hills around Cobalt and the sites of the many mines that operated there. Prepared by the Mining Museum and the Ontario government, the tour is a well-marked self-guiding drive. Start by driving east on Lang Street from the firefighters' museum.

Proceed a short distance to Ferland Street and, at the Miner's Tavern, turn right. Across the wooden bridge over the railway tracks stands the rusting headframe of the Right of Way Mine (so-called because it sits on the railway right-of-way), where three million ounces of silver were extracted. Here, where silver was mined from beneath the railway track, you will see a display of ancient mining machinery. Just beyond the bridge and on the left stands the legendary LaRose Blacksmith Shop where, legend has it, blacksmith Fred LaRose flung an axe at a fox. The axe chipped a rock, exposing what would become one the camp's richest ore bodies.

From the blacksmith's shop follow Kerr Lake Road, as it is called here, to Cross Lake Road, keeping right on Kerr Lake Road. This brings you to the Colonial Mine where you can arrange a tour with the mining museum. The route continues past the Nova Scotia Mine and mill site where operations ended in 1921. Just beyond the junction with Glenn Lake Road you will encounter one of Cobalt's more legendary mines, the Silver Sidewalk. The vein was literally the width of a sidewalk

The headframe from the former Buffalo Mine was used to keep produce cool when it was converted to a grocery store.

but plunged deep into the ground, as you will see from the viewing platform. From this location, the Beaver Temisk Road and the Penn Mill Road lead to other mine sites, where headframes yet loom above the forests—although these locations are not in the guidebook

Return to town by following the Kerr Lake Road back to the Glenn Lake Road and then Coleman Road. This will lead you to the McKinley Darragh mine site, where the town's first mill clanged into operation in 1903. A viewing platform here offers a look at the extensive ruins. The Coleman Road comes to a stop sign on Highway 11B, where a turn to the right leads back into town. The headframe that guards the entrance to the town here is the headframe and shaft for the Townsite Mine. Park here and follow the path to the "Glory Hole," which gives you a glimpse into an open

pit. Highway 11B leads you back to the mining museum. Overnight accommodation is available at the Silverland Motel on Lang Street beside which is Brooksy's Restaurant for a family-style meal.

## Side Trip to Silver Centre

This section of the route leaves behind the scarred hillsides of Cobalt and leads you through a lush hidden valley with high, wooded hillsides and a valley floor of pastures and fields. Follow Highway 11B east from Cobalt for 4 km to Highway 567.

Turn right onto Highway 567 and follow it southeast through the rugged little village of North Cobalt and into a landscape of a rock and forest. After 7 km, the road bends south and enters the Lorrain Valley. The gentle pastoral scenes that you see during the next 20 km contrast starkly with the hard, forbidding bedrock that surrounds you.

At about 18 km from Highway 11B, a historical marker points down Old Mission Road to the shores of Lake Timiskaming and the site of an Oblate mission established in 1863 and now long-vanished. To continue on your southerly route, return to Highway 567 and turn left. After passing more farms and fields for 7 km, the road rises out of the valley onto a rocky plateau. A little over 2 km from the last group of buildings on the left, look for a cindered road that branches right from Highway 567. This is the road to the ghost town of Silver Centre.

## Silver Centre

As the Cobalt boom neared its peak in 1907, prospectors ventured farther afield and, in that year, discovered silver in these remote hills. Other mines quickly moved in, and the town of Silver Centre grew to a population of 700 with a streetcar connection to Cobalt and a hockey team of its own. Of the two dozen mines that worked the area, however, fewer than a half-dozen were profitable. By 1930 the silver boom had faded, and so had Silver Centre. As the mines closed, the rails were lifted and the road fell into disrepair.

Here, in 1925, you would have found stores and shops, a school, a theatre, a hockey rink, 50 houses and cabins and assorted mine structures. Silver Centre at its peak was home to 700 people. Sadly, the buildings were all moved or burned, and the regenerating forest hides most of what's left.

## Silver Centre to Matabitchuan

From Silver Centre, Highway 567 continues another 13 km to its end at the Matabitchuan

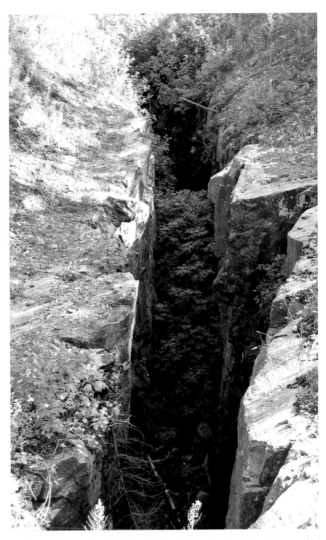

Visitors can now view the Silver Sidewalk, thanks to a drive-it-yourself tour route.

Dam. For 9 km the road winds across the forested highland that repulsed any efforts to settle it. Then it suddenly emerges from the woods and crosses a modern bridge. The lake to your right is the forebay for the Lower Notch Generating Station. The massive dam and powerhouse lie to your left, but are not clearly visible from the road. The pond created behind the dam backs 15 km up the Montreal River.

# 21 The Trail of the Sleeping Giant

A lake in Sleeping Giant National Park.

Ontario's most famous rock formation is for many the Sleeping Giant of Thunder Bay. Arms folded across its chest, the figure consists of ancient limestone mesas that shape the Sibley Peninsula southeast of that Lakehead city. This trip uncovers the mysteries of the Sleeping Giant and probes the farming and fishing communities of this remote finger of land.

The route starts at Pearl on the Trans-Canada Highway, 50 km east of Thunder Bay, and runs south down the Sibley Peninsula and back for about 100 km.

This journey is for the hiker, the photographer and the ghost-town lover. Former fishing villages (reminiscent of the much-photographed Peggy's Cove in Nova Scotia) indent the east coast of the peninsula. Through the Sleeping Giant Provincial Park, the authorities have cut hiking trails to the lofty head and chest of the Sleeping Giant; and at the remote tip of the peninsula sits the site of Ontario's oldest, and richest, silver discovery—the ghost town of Silver Islet.

n 1845, silver was discovered on a small rocky islet 2 km off the tip of the Sibley Peninsula and it became the focus for the first European settlement in the area. Then in the mid-1880s the Canadian Pacific Railway hammered its rails across the neck of the peninsula. It was followed in 1903 by the Canadian Northern Railway, which paralleled it a few kilometres south. From the station villages of Pearl and Pass Lake, bush trails extended down the peninsula. Commercial fishing had been in full swing along the American shore since the fur-trading days of the 1820s and 1830s, but now the railways provided a means of shipping out the local catch. Soon most of the coves that could harbour a tug or a few skiffs had a small fishing station.

Farm settlement progressed much more slowly. Bush farms along the road to the railway stations gave way after the First World War to a settlement scheme to open up the peninsula's fertile post-glacial deposits near Pass Lake. It was to this plain in 1924 that the Ontario government invited 65 Danish settlers.

Although there were fewer farmers than fishermen, their activities are still evident on much of the peninsula's landscape. Tourism, however, has surpassed both farming and fishing as travellers pick through the amethyst mines near Pearl, hike the trails of the provincial park or settle for the summer into the miners' cabins in a ghost town.

## Pearl to Johnsons Landing

The first portion of the route follows a one-time bush trail from Pearl, passes some bush farms and then leads into Johnsons Landing, the Peggy's Cove of the peninsula. From Pearl, drive south on Road 5. After less than 1 km, the road crosses the abandoned CNR right-of-way and then for 1 km follows the Pearl River, more a creek than a river. Along its banks you may see evidence of the early farms. The

Johnson Harbour is one of several attractive fishing coves on the Sibley Peninsula.

road then swings south and traverses a low, rolling landscape of young forest and overgrown clearings. Here the pockets of soil were small and infertile, and the bush farms were soon abandoned.

After 9 km, you will come to a T intersection. Your route lies to the right, but first turn left for a short trip to Johnsons Landing, reminiscent of Canada's maritime fishing villages perched on the smooth rocks that ring the small bay. Beyond the wooded inlet are the waters of Black Bay, a wide indentation of Lake Superior that contains some of the lake's best fishing.

## Johnsons Landing to Silver Islet

The next section of the route leads through the prosperous Danish settlement to Squaw Bay, then through the Sleeping Giant Provincial Park to the legendary Silver Islet.

From the dead end at Johnsons Landing, return the way you came, and then turn left at the intersection. Suddenly the wide, level plain of the Danish farming community appears from the bush. Farm enlargements and abandonment of the fringe area have reduced the dozen and a half original farms to the half-dozen that carry on today.

From the first crossroads that you come to the road traverses the fertile farmland and, after 2 km, crosses a narrow wooden bridge. Look for a side road 1 km beyond the bridge. This side road, the Pass Lake Crossroad, leads west to Highway 587, the route you will take on your return. For the present, continue straight ahead. After 1 km, the road leaves the last of the farms and returns to Crown land. The road then continues to follow the bay. Summer cottages mingle with fishermen's cabins and even with the clearings of early farms.

Another 2 km bring you to the boundary of the Sleeping Giant Provincial Park, and, after a further 1 km, you come to a stop sign at Highway 587. Turn left to reach the campgrounds and trails for which the park has become famous.

At 3 km from the turn you will see on your right the starting point of a scenic drive through the park that provides you with spectacular views from the top of the mesa. The mesa is one of a group of mesas that forms the park's most famous feature, the Sleeping Giant.

Ojibwa legend claims that the shape is the form of a chief named Nanabozo (or Nanabijou), who was the son of the west wind. The chief had led his people to the peninsula to keep them safe from their traditional enemy, the Sioux, and it was here on a tiny rock shoal that they discovered silver. But to reveal its location, especially to the Europeans, meant retribution from the Great Spirit, so the chief swore his followers to secrecy. However, one of his subchiefs had secretly made jewellery from

the metal, and, after the Sioux had captured him in battle, they led a group of Europeans to the islet. When the chief saw them coming, he called up a storm to send the canoes and their travellers to the cold depths of the lake. In punishment the Great Spirit turned Nanabozo to stone, the Sleeping Giant.

Geologists, however, have come up with a decidedly less colourful explanation. The rock mesa, they claim, is simply the remnant of a great limestone plateau whose sediments were laid down by an ancient sea. No matter how it got there, Ontario's most spectacular hiking trails lead to its lofty summits. To reach them, continue 12 km south on Highway 587 and ask for trail maps in the park office.

From the peaks of the mesa that tower here, 140 metres above the grey waters of the lake, you can see grain ships gliding in and out of Thunder Bay harbour, the wooded shoreline below and, in the distance, the shapes of other mesas.

**Some surprisingly fertile soils attracted a colony of Danes to the Sibley Peninsula.**

The main street of the ghost mining town of Silver Islet has changed little since its mine closed, although many of the cabins have become summer homes.

## Silver Islet

From the park continue south on the highway. After 3 km, the road leaves the woods and enters a clearing. Then, in a long row, the cabins of the 100-year-old village of Silver Islet appear.

This was the site of Canada's richest silver strike. It all began in 1845 when Joseph Woods, who was exploring for copper, discovered an unusually rich silver vein on a rocky shoal 2 km from the tip of the peninsula. But there was no economical means of transporting the ore, and it lay idle until 1870, when Major William Sibley of Detroit bought the claim for what would be the bargain price of $250,000. He hired an engineer named William Frue to build retaining walls and to bring the mine into production. It seemed the spirit of Nanabozo grew restless and sent storms, tidal waves and ice to destroy Frue's breakwaters.

However, by 1873 Frue had constructed a barrier that withstood all that the Sleeping Giant could hurl at it, and production began.

On the islet Frue placed the mine buildings and bunkhouses; on the shore, a stamping mill with 50 stamps; and extending along a 2 km shoreline, 40 houses, a hotel, two churches, a store and a log jail. Within ten years, production exceeded $3 million, a figure that made it Canada's richest silver mine.

As the shafts edged out under the floor of the lake, huge coal-filled boilers were installed to pump out the perpetual leaks. By 1884 the peninsula had no more logs to feed the flames of the pumps, and all eyes looked southward for the form of the winter coal boat. The anxious residents could scarcely have known that, far over the horizon, the boat's captain, inebriated, had run the ship fast aground. Before he could free her, an early freeze clamped the vessel in ice for the winter. Silver Islet would get no coal. By March the flames in the boilers died and water began to fill the shafts. The mine was finished.

Miraculously, the town survived. Soon after the miners had fled, residents of the growing towns of Port Arthur and Fort William (the twin cities that are today's Thunder Bay) bought up the cabins as summer homes. Since then, successive owners have preserved, and in some cases replaced, the buildings of the town. The only structures to disappear are the mill, the mine buildings on the islet, the Catholic church, and the mansion of the mine's owner, Major Sibley.

As you enter the village, the first building you see is the log jail. It is Ontario's only surviving log jail and is privately preserved. Then the road enters the village proper and leads straight to the massive wooden store, now restored as a residence. From it the old miners' cabins, along with newer cottages, stretch along the shore. Their sturdy construction, and their distance from one another—a fire prevention measure—have combined to ensure their longevity.

Highway 587, more a lane, follows the shoreline to the left of the store. Still narrow, much as the miners might remember it, it is a one-way route during the summer. Follow the road east along the shore. Lake Superior laps at your right, while the miners' cabins line the road on your left. As the road swings inland, the miners' graveyard lies about 100 metres into the bush to your left. To your right, far off the shore, you may be able to discern the low form of the shoal that produced Canada's richest silver mine.

## Silver Islet to Pass Lake

The last segment of the route returns up the peninsula along a clifftop drive to the hamlet of Pass Lake. From there you can continue to the

The town cemetery for the ghost town of Silver Islet, abandoned a century ago. It is now a cottage community at the tip of the Sibley Peninsula.

deep Ouimet Canyon or to some of Canada's best amethyst-gathering sites.

About 1 km after the one-way road through Silver Islet leaves the shore, it reconnects with the two-way Highway 587. To return north, turn right and travel 30 km to Pass Lake. Alternatively, if it is open, you can embark on a scenic side trip to the park's clifftops.

## Sleeping Giant Side Trip

Back at Sleeping Giant Park, the 15 km scenic side route leaves the highway and twists across a rough and rocky terrain to the clifftops of the Sleeping Giant. Here, 150 km above the lake, it follows the cliffs. At three locations there are specially cleared viewpoints. From them you can see the wooded Caribou Island and the coastline of Lake Superior as it curves toward the city of Thunder Bay.

After the road reconnects with Highway 587, Pass Lake village lies 1 km to your right. Pass Lake, originally a station on the Canadian Northern

The Pass Lake railway trestle is among Ontario's loftiest railway bridges.

Railway, became the focus for the Danish farm colony to its east, which was at one time famous for its strawberries. Seventy thousand quarts were shipped from the station in 1935 alone. Today the village contains the squat, white Salem Lutheran Church that dates from the Danish migration, and Karen's Kountry Kitchen on the lake (opposite the abandoned railway right-of-way). The restaurant is the former station master's house. A few kilometres north you pass beneath the same rail, only here it hovers high above the roadway on what is northern Ontario's highest railway trestle.

## More to See

A drive of 5 km north brings you back to the Trans-Canada Highway.

Canada's best amethyst deposits lie a few kilometres east. Most are privately owned, and the owners will allow you to collect on your own for a fee. The best pieces, however, usually make their way to the on-site gift shops first. To visit an operating mine complete with tours and a gift shop, follow Highway 17 east to East Loon Lake Road and follow the directions to the Panorama Mine. The views along this long and twisting route give a clue as to how this interesting mine earned its name.

## Side Trip to a "Grand Canyon"

You may also explore Ontario's own Grand Canyon. Ouimet Canyon is a 5 km long fissure that plunges 100 metres down into the ancient bedrock. So little sunlight reaches the bottom of the canyon that rare types of arctic vegetation—survivors of the ice age—grow undisturbed. To reach the canyon, drive east from Pearl for 10 km to the Ouimet Canyon Road and follow the Ouimet Canyon

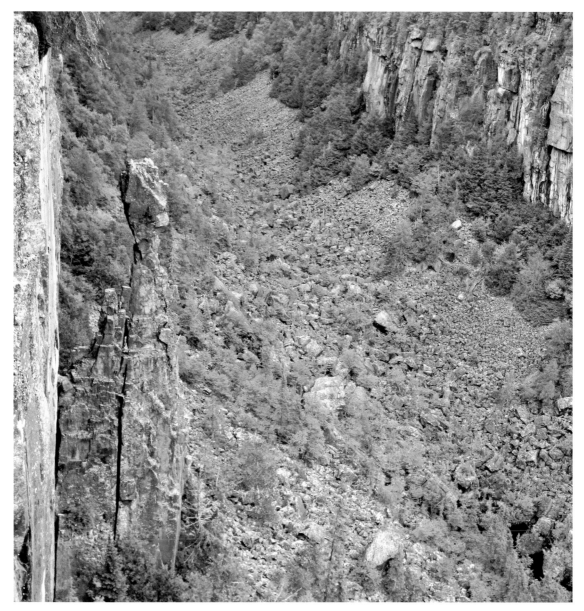

Indian Head at Ouimet Canyon Provincial Park.

Provincial Park signs for another 10 km. This free park contains several kilometres of hiking trails, but be careful. There are few guardrails, and the footing can be slippery.

For a more interactive canyon adventure, follow the signs along the Ouimet Canyon Road to Eagle Canyon, where two suspension foot bridges, including Canada's longest at 200 metres, suspends you more than 50 metres above the yawning canyon.

**Overleaf: This suspension bridge crosses Eagle Canyon near Ouimet Canyon.**

# 22 The Silver Mountain Road

West of the city of Thunder Bay lies a range of mountains that the Ojibwa call the Shuniah Weachu—Mountains of Silver. A series of soaring flat-top mesas, they spawned one of Ontario's first silver rushes. This 80 km route winds beneath their looming cliffs, taking you not only to the early silver mines, but also to waterfalls and valley villages, northwestern Ontario's first Finnish settlement, and a peek at the Ghost Railway to Nowhere.

The route starts at Kakabeka Falls, 30 km west of Thunder

The Kakabeka Falls on the Kaministiquia River are easily accessible for cars and campers.

Bay on the Trans-Canada Highway 17, and follows paved secondary highways to Middle Falls, on the historic Pigeon River, Canada's boundary with the United States.

The early history of the Thunder Bay area is one of fur trading. Fort William began as a North West Company fur post in the closing years of the 18th century and became one of Ontario's largest trading posts. The fort has been carefully reconstructed, albeit on a different site, as a living museum. Its neighbour on the shore of Lake Superior, Prince Arthur's Landing, grew into a port where schooners called for furs and fish. In the 1880s, when the Canadian Pacific Railway was being constructed northwest from Lake Superior, these settlements grew into the towns of Fort William and Port Arthur. Nine decades later, they would amalgamate as the city of Thunder Bay. Thunder Bay is the highest city in Ontario's North, and is Ontario's tenth largest.

But the wealth of the fur was soon eclipsed by something far more spectacular—silver. In 1882, a local Ojibwa chief, Joseph L'Avocat, led prospector Oliver Daunais to the secret silver veins west of Thunder Bay, riches that until then the Native people had kept as closely guarded secrets. But the word got out, and the rush was on. Over the next 20 years, nearly a dozen mining camps were built in the mountains of silver. The largest were the twin towns of Silver Mountain East End and Silver Mountain West End. To gain access to them, the Silver Mountain Highway was built into the area, followed in 1891 by a little railway called the Port Arthur Duluth & Western (PDW) Railway but more fittingly nicknamed the "Poverty Agony Distress and Welfare" line. But the deposits were meagre and production disappointing. By 1910, the mines were silent.

When the mines closed, many of the miners, most of them immigrants from Finland, stayed on to clear small bush farms along the Silver Mountain Road. Others followed, expanding the clearings and lending the area a flavour of old Finland with distinctive Finnish barn and house styles. Even as recently as the 1920s, new land was being broken along the Pigeon River, making the area one of Ontario's last true frontiers.

## Kakabeka Falls to Hymers

This trip begins at a waterfall that has been called the Niagara of the North, and then follows the Silver Mountains to an obscure railway town. Well known to the early fur traders and Indians, Kakabeka Falls was the first difficult portage on the Kaministikwia River fur highway. Here, 30 km west of Lake Superior, the Kam drops 39 metres over a hard granite brink. Erosion has carved a gorge 3 km from the original lip of the escarpment. Beside the thundering cataract is a park that contains trails which follow the ancient portages used by Native peoples and, later, the voyageurs. The legend of Green Mantle tells of an Ojibwa princess, held by invading Sioux warriors, who led her captors over the brink of the falls to their deaths, and her own demise as well.

From the park, drive east on the Trans-Canada Highway for 4 km to Highway 588 and then turn south. The next 2 km lead you down the wall of the Kam Valley to a hamlet called Stanley. Once a busy junction on the PDW, Stanley can boast a pair of buildings that date from those steam-filled days. Along the north side of the river the rails have long been lifted, and Rosslyn Road follows the former rail bed.

Your route takes you south over the Kam River, where you will see a few of the prosperous farms on the silty soils of the river's flood plain. Across the bridge, at a T intersection, Highway 588 turns right to follow the old Silver Mountain Highway. Although it bears no resemblance to the bush trail first carved into the forests in the 1890s, Highway 588 still follows the route along the foot of the great mesas. After 3 km, the peaks loom close on your left. On your right are the small overgrown clearings of the area's first bush farmers; some of them now contain the modern homes of the area's country dwellers.

At 12 km west from the Kam River bridge, you will enter Hymers. Originally a station on the PDW, it grew into a busy service town for the pioneer community. But when the railway closed here in 1954 and when better roads made Port Arthur and Fort William more accessible, many residents left. Today, without the newer homes of Thunder Bay's commuters, Hymers would be a ghost town.

To enter Hymers, turn right from 588 onto Highway 595 and drive down the wall of the Whitefish River Valley into the village. Before the bridge is a wooden mansion that was home to the family after whom the town was named. Across the small bridge is the village museum, housed in a wooden building that was originally the United church. The museum has displays of early pioneer implements, along with photographs of the town in its heyday. A few metres beyond the museum, Highway 595 turns right. This is the town's main intersection, where five stores, three blacksmith shops, two boarding houses and the PDW railway station once stood, giving the street its current name, Pee Dee Road.

## Hymers to Nolalu

The next section of the route leaves Highway 588 to trace the original Silver Mountain Highway beneath red cliffs and into northwestern Ontario's Little Finland.

From the centre of Hymers, return to Highway 588, turn right and drive 5.5 km. Here at a stop sign the highway turns sharply right, while the Old Silver Mountain Highway follows a dirt road straight ahead. Follow the old road. This narrow trail winds past bush farms, many of which were started by unemployed miners on poor soils and

**An early Finnish farmstead west of Thunder Bay.**

are now sporting a few new country homes. Then the road swings into the shadow of a high, rocky mesa, which, with its vertical columns of rock, is called the Palisades.

After 5 km, you will come to a crossroad. Ahead of you, the old Silver Mountain route continues for another 1.5 km and then becomes passable only by four-wheel-drive vehicles. So you should turn right at the crossroads, crossing the bridge over the Silver Falls Creek. On this wide, sandy plain, a dozen Finnish farms—their barns still displaying distinctive round roofs—once operated.

After travelling 4 km from the crossroads, you will enter the valley of the Whitefish River once again and arrive at Nolalu. Originally a station on the PDW, its odd name came not from a town in far-off Finland, as many have surmised, but rather for its first postmaster, who named it after

his lumber company, North Land Lumber (hence, No-La-Lu). The single village street beside the highway once shaded the railway track. Trains called three times a week, and the village became the focus for the Finnish farm community that surrounded it. Despite a decline in the rural population after the closing of the railway, the village has remained almost totally Finnish.

The PDW began as a Port Arthur effort to link with the coveted Canadian Pacific Railway in Fort William. Despite being thwarted by the CPR, its promoters built the line beyond Fort William and onward to the border with Minnesota, where they had expected to link with an American line proposed from Duluth. The American link was never built, and the PDW ended, literally, in the middle of nowhere.

A log chute by the falls on the Pigeon River.

## Nolalu to Silver Mountain

The next section of your route follows the rail bed of the PDW, winding along the valley of the Whitefish River to Shuniah Weachu, the Mountain of Silver. From Nolalu, turn west onto Highway 588 and drive out of the village. More small bush farms peer from the young woodlots here. Although new country homes of commuters to Thunder Bay have replaced some the early farm homes, you may yet see examples of early Finnish houses and barns.

On the southwest corner of the junction with Highway 593 is the site of Silver Mountain station. Now a restaurant, its pyramid roof exemplifies a pattern devised by the PDW's later owners, the Canadian Northern Railway. Turn left here onto Highway 593.

Looming above the plain on the southeastern horizon is Silver Mountain itself. It was on this summit between 1890 and 1910 that the twin silver towns of Silver Mountain East End and Silver Mountain West End grew. Each contained not only mines and mills, but also hotels, stores and two dozen log cabins. But the mining activity was only sporadic; by 1910 it had ceased and the villages vanished.

Your route now ventures into a remote part of Ontario that was one of the province's last frontiers. Over the next 5 km, Highway 593 skirts the west end of the mountain and then enters the canyon of the Little Whitefish River. After 8 km, the river tumbles beside the road. After a few more kilometres, Highway 593 crosses the Arrow River, where the rural settlement of Jackpine is clustered. For

Opposite: On a cold day ice is forming from the water mist and covering everything around the High Falls waterfall on the Pigeon River.

Now a popular restaurant, the Silver Mountain station is the last to linger on the ill-fated PDW rail line.

the next 20 km the highway follows the valley of the Arrow River

Until the First World War, the valley of the Arrow River was unknown to all but a few trappers and loggers. But surveys showed a wide, apparently fertile, valley floor that could become a new farming community. Then, in the late 1920s and the early 1930s, with the Depression in full gear and bread lines growing in the cities of the south, the Ontario government threw open the flat soils of Devon Township to settlers. Many of the settlers were Finns, attracted by the proximity of the Finnish colonies of Suomi and Nolalu. Other settlers were simply trying to escape the Depression.

The last section of your route continues down the valley of the Arrow River and ends amid the spectacular mountains and waterfalls that mark the Pigeon River.

From the bridge over the Arrow River continue on Highway 593. For 5 km the road crosses the flat flood plain of the valley where overgrown clearings that mark failed efforts at farming are being overtaken by a young regenerating forest. The road then crosses the river once more and traverses a rolling, rocky countryside where the clearings of the bush farms become farther apart. After 10 km, at a T intersection, Highway 593 turns left, and the Old Pigeon River Road leads right for 2 km to the abandoned border crossing of Pigeon River.

The recorded history of the Pigeon River dates from the fur-trading days, when it was the highway to the west. Fur seekers, both French and Native peoples, paddled upstream to the fur grounds and returned laden with skins. But after the American Revolution, the Pigeon River became the new international border. Threats of customs duties forced the fur trappers to the Kam River, a more difficult route, but one that was free of international wrangling.

The area's first road had been built in the 1880s to bring mail from Duluth to the silver mines, but once the railways assumed this function the road fell into disrepair. It took until 1915 and angry petitions from area settlers to improve the road, but there was still no bridge. Rotary clubs in the Lakehead cities collected money to bridge the chasm, but because they had failed to complete an international agreement for the crossing, the bridge was dubbed the Outlaw Bridge.

Years later, during the 1950s and 1960s, when highways across Ontario were widened and improved, the westerly crossing of the Pigeon River was abandoned in favour of a new alignment 10 km east. The customs buildings were dismantled and moved. Among the foundations and vacant lots, fewer than a half-dozen buildings remain at the old crossing. And the Outlaw Bridge has vanished forever.

Return to Highway 593 and follow it east to Highway 61. The road crosses another rocky plain and for 6 km follows the north bank of the Pigeon River and the entrance to Pigeon River Provincial Park, with its soaring mesas and hiking trails, to the more spectacular 30-metre-high Pigeon Falls. Trails also lead to Middle Falls. Although the falls are only 15 metres high, they are wide and the water thunders furiously into the eddies below. Portions of a rare early timber chute lie beside the falls. The Pigeon River is part of the Canadian Heritage River System Boundary Waters Voyageur Waterway.

Highway 593 ends at Highway 61. And so your route ends as it began, near some of Ontario's most picturesque waterfalls and amid some of its most magnificent mountain scenery. The highway will return you north to Thunder Bay, while the American border lies about 2 km south.

# Index of Cities, Towns, Villages and Hamlets

# Index

# Photo Credits

All photographs are courtesy of the author, Ron Brown, except for the following:

Cover: Top - StudioNewmarket/Shutterstock.com; Bottom - mlorenz/Shutterstock.com

Back cover: 2nd row left - Christopher Meder/Shutterstock.com; Bottom - David P. Lewis/Shutterstock.com

Pg 2: mlorenz/Shutterstock.com

Pg 5: Chris Collins/Shutterstock.com

Pg 6: © iStockphoto.com

Pg 8: David P. Lewis/Shutterstock.com

Pg 10: Elena Elisseeva/Shutterstock.com

Pg 13: SF photo/Shutterstock.com

Pg 24: SF photo/Shutterstock.com

Pg 27: SF photo/Shutterstock.com

Pg 29: SF photo/Shutterstock.com

Pg 38: Christopher Meder/Shutterstock.com

Pg 40: Mark52/Shutterstock.com

Pg 47: Viktorus/Shutterstock.com

Pg 55: © George Fischer Photography

Pg 59: SF photo/Shutterstock.com

Pg 77: pavels/Shutterstock.com

Pg 85: SF photo/Shutterstock.com

Pgs 88-89: © iStockphoto.com

Pgs 98-99: © iStockphoto.com

Pg 112: SF photo/Shutterstock.com

Pg 122: SF photo/Shutterstock.com

Pg 131: David P. Lewis/Shutterstock.com

Pg 132: Leo Bruce/Dreamstime.com

Pg 134: Paul McKinnon/Shutterstock.com

Pg 136: Paul McKinnon/Shutterstock.com

Pgs 140-41: David P. Lewis/Shutterstock.com

Pg 159: © George Fischer Photography

Pg 165: Pavelshe/Dreamstime.com

Pg 171: Meg Wallace Photography/Shutterstock.com

Pg 173: Judy Tiessen/Dreamstime.com

Pgs 176-77: © iStockphoto.com/gladassfanny

Pg 178: John Goldstein/Shutterstock.com

Pg 183: SF photo/Shutterstock.com

Pgs 186-87: Christopher Meder/Shutterstock.com

Pg 194: pavels/Shutterstock.com

Pg 201: David P. Lewis/Shutterstock.com

Pgs 202-03: Wolf Mountain Images/Shutterstock.com

Pg 204: © Hartley Millson

Pg 209: Owl Mountain/Shutterstock.com